Thank you
for reading!
TJ Butler

Dating Silky Maxwell

Stories by

TJ Butler

ISBN: 978-1-942004-62-2

Library of Congress Control Number: 2023946703

Cover Art by Charles Butler
Cover Design by ELJ Editions, Ltd.

ELJ Editions, Ltd.
P.O. Box 815
Washingtonville, NY 10992

www.elj-editions.com

Praise for *Dating Silky Maxwell*

"Butler communicates the stories of these women in clear, unadorned prose, which allows her to focus on potent symbols of resistance and resilience. These are deceptively simple tales, told in accessible and insightful ways."

—*Kirkus Review*

"There's so much to love about these stories, but it's the characters who've been haunting me, vivid and flawed and human and as beautifully written as any I've met in life."

—Amber Sparks, author of *And I Do Not Forgive You*, named Best Book of 2020 by The Washington Post, NPR, Bustle, Good Housekeeping, and Tor.com

"*Dating Silky Maxwell* introduces readers to an important new voice. TJ Butler's poignant collection about uneasy lives will be well-remembered long after you close this exquisite volume that hauntingly touches both the heart and mind."

—Pete Earley, Pulitzer Prize finalist author of *Crazy: A Father's Search Through America's Mental Health Madness*

For my husband, Charles.
Writing this book would not have been possible without you.

Poppy, I wrote a book!

Contents

The Wings That Follow Fear

Two nights before Ryder's coming home day, I walked down the hill to the barn to say goodnight to the animals. My hair was hanging loose over my thin cotton nightgown, the long plain one I wear in the summer when he's gone. The air was soft and still. The field beyond the barn twinkled with lightning bugs like a scene in a movie. I walked past the barn to the edge of the field, picked out one glowing flash, still and low to the ground. I counted the morse code of brilliance that flared in a pulsing yes to entice a mate. I thought of Ryder as I turned toward the barn, wishing for his hand in mine on the edge of this field, longing to watch the flickering display with him.

I plucked his old plaid shirt from the nail by the barn door. I'd worn it so many times since he'd been gone that it smelled more of me than him. I could not get closer to him than the flannel sleeves around my arms, but I did not mind. His coming home day was so close. As I slipped my arms into the soft, worn sleeves, I heard the faraway crunch of tires on our gravel drive.

I stepped out of the barn, heart pounding deep inside my chest. Ryder was not due home for a couple of days, but he was prone to surprise me occasionally. I was a sight in his shirt, my nightgown hanging like a sack, my scuffed, brown work boots unlaced with smears of red clay mud along the soles. I'd been planning a homecoming that smelled of roasted chicken and apple pie, a dinner softly lit to golden by the sun dropping low behind the trees that marked our property line. To have him home a few days early, I'd take what I could get, whether it was in the barn, in the house, or in a field in the back forty.

The headlights were too low to be Ryder's aging Silverado. I did not have other family left, or many friends in town, and none would have visited at this hour. I buttoned the plaid shirt over my nightgown and stood with my arms crossed over my chest, tense and coiled. I watched the car creeping along the drive until it stopped in front of the barn. It was a Cadillac, spotted with rust and peeling paint, and missing the driver's side mirror. I waited for the driver to emerge, but the engine continued to run. The headlights illuminated the land beyond the barn, filling the brilliant sparkling field with a sickly, yellow glow. I paused for a few breaths, wishing I'd stepped inside the barn for the shotgun before the car got this close. If the driver were lost, I'd send them just past town to the gas station that was open until midnight. If the driver was not lost… I did not pause to consider that option. Ryder was not in this car, and no one else had any cause to come out this way.

I could almost feel the smooth wooden stock of the shotgun in my hands. Its absence was tangible. I stepped toward the Cadillac, feigning confidence I did not feel while imagining the power of the single shell in the shotgun's chamber. I faced demons unarmed in my own kitchen as a girl. I could do it again as a woman, but I still hoped I could send the driver on their way with a nod toward the gas station.

"Well, if it isn't Louisa Eaton!" A man's voice called out from behind the wheel as he cut the engine. I recognized the voice, but I could not immediately place it. I uncoiled slightly, exhaled, and took another step toward the car to try to see the driver. He called out again, "Hey there, Lou! It's been an age."

My heart sank as I recognized him, identifying his thick mop of dishwater blond curls as Billy Ricketts. We were in the same grade until he left school before graduation to finish out the year in a boy's reformatory upstate. He was locked up more than he was home as an adult, and I'd heard his rap sheet included armed robbery and attempted murder. In between stints behind bars, he was either fixing to steal someone's wife or hanging around The Horseshoe cheating at pool and then picking fights in the parking lot.

His voice was too friendly, a used car salesman peddling a lemon that wouldn't start, rather than a long-ago acquaintance showing up uninvited after dark.

"What're you doing out here, Billy? You need something?"

Next was me coiling just a bit tighter as he unfolded himself from the driver's seat and leaned against the door. I took a step away from him. I was tall, with childbearing hips and all the other platitudes women say to girls who suddenly shoot up and fill out as their adult forms are revealed. I could hold my own with the land and the animals and keep the wood stove filled, but he was taller, broader. He was verging on handsome in a fitted white tee shirt and faded jeans, a cowboy who appealed to girls who preferred wearing boots to high heels. He ran a hand through his hair, preening and unhurried.

He made eye contact with me in the dimming twilight, and his voice was as casual as two old school friends catching up. "Aw, Lou, I've just come to say hello. Can't a man stop by to see an old friend?" I did not respond. He continued, saying he'd heard in town about Ryder's job, said I must be lonesome all the way out here by myself. His eyes traveled from my face to my brown work boots and back. He drawled that my hair had gotten pretty long, said I must be hot with that ragged shirt buttoned so far up.

I felt a stone form in my stomach. I repeated my question, "You need something?" I knew he did not stop by my place at night to see how long my hair had grown.

"What do I need, Lou? How about I need to lay low for a while…" The rest of his words lost the shape of language, but I heard these things: armed robbery… roadblocks… just until the county roads are clear to the state line. My mind raced with an old, familiar fear. Time slowed, but my thoughts whirled and spun like a centrifuge. It had been decades since I had to make plans against a man set on doing a woman harm. I'd been out of practice for years; my daddy was long gone. I did not live that life with Ryder, but here I was.

Billy Ricketts did not know when Ryder was due home. His wary laying-low presence was a hairpin trigger, a trap Ryder would walk into unaware and unarmed while Billy Ricketts was already watchful and anxious. I could not let that happen to my man.

Just beyond my fear, small hummingbird wings of self-preservation fluttered furiously. Men enraged, drunk, or in pain are wildly unpredictable. In their frenzy, they often underestimate their targets. If I could outmaneuver this man, even for a moment, I had a chance. I clenched my shaking hands into fists, but I could not calm myself. I was the only thing standing in the way of Billy Ricketts laying low on my property without incident.

I cursed myself for idly watching a stranger's car crawl down the driveway instead of taking five steps inside the barn for the shotgun. I had nothing on under my nightgown, and my unlaced boots were too loose to support a sprint through the fields to the forest beyond. He had come here to help himself to my land and bide his time for as long as he pleased.

He walked toward me. His voice had a smooth, honeyed tone. "You wouldn't mind helping out an old friend for a while, would you? Let's go take a walk in the field, Lou." Crickets chirped. I could hear a dog barking in the distance. Thoughts flashed in my mind, images more than articulation. If I let him lead me into the field, I'd never make it back. The turkey vultures would find me before anyone else, and he'd make himself at home until Ryder drove his old Silverado down the gravel drive. The wings of hope that shadowed my fear beat desperately, just beyond my grasp. If I walked into the tall grasses beyond the barn, my house would never smell like the first home-cooked meal Ryder had eaten in months. I saw the list of chores I didn't get done as urgent sparks; the fencepost, the squeaking door, the yellow jacket nest in the barn.

Billy Ricketts approached me with extended hands, a dark, threatening silhouette against the deepening navy of the sky. His lips curled into a wolfish smile, a hungry carnivore purporting to a rabbit that it wants to pet them, not devour them. The chores flared in my mind again. The yellow jacket's nest was a sudden shock of heat lightning, an epiphany, a bombshell. Billy Ricketts had never met a woman who bit back.

§

His hand shot out, fingers circling my wrist. My breath caught in my chest. I felt the wings that follow fear, but I had no time to consider their message. As a girl, I did not always know what to do when the seconds ticked toward an inevitable danger. This time, the fingers circling my wrist released an instinct without vocabulary. I followed it without thinking. I tilted my head upwards, looking through my lashes at him, forced myself to be passive and pliant as a doe. My voice was low and breathy. "Come on into the barn with me, Billy." I placed my free hand on his hand that held my wrist, and I was surprised when he allowed it. My tongue darted to the corner of my mouth. It was dangerous to push this far, to suggest an intimacy and interrupt the reason he'd come to my place. I left my lips parted. I gazed at him, feeling nauseous at the insinuation. I could do no more than plant a seed. I wanted to stop there. Instead, I imagined the finality of walking into the field. I turned toward the barn without hesitating. I'd have to let him finish up what I started. He followed me into the barn. I turned on the lights as we entered, then slid the door closed. The latch was tricky to open, a death sentence for one of us if it stuck, and a death sentence for the other if it did not.

The corners beneath the hayloft were dark. He spoke, but I did not turn to look at him. I exhaled slowly, willed myself into an easy victim for this one grand action. He stopped in front of the horse stalls. He pulled me backward, bent to force his mouth onto mine. I wrenched my head away, crying out words that made no sense, "The horses!" He cursed, pushed me to the floor.

I scrambled to my feet. His body tensed, prepared to spring if I moved. He no longer trusted me. He spat sharp-edged words that did not matter. The used car salesman was gone. I turned my face toward him and pointed toward the bales of hay beneath the hayloft. I needed the darkness, the low eaves, and the opportunity. I did not know how to command a predator, but I'd extended an invitation he was now impatient to take me up on.

He grabbed my arm and strode forward, long legs pulling me toward the hay beneath the overhang. He spun me around, moving quickly, pressing me against the wall with his shoulder. I was silent and still, allowing his hands to roam freely. He grunted as he reached down to pull my nightgown up with one hand and unbuckle his belt with the other. I turned my head away from him, focusing on the yellow jacket nest. It was easy to miss, a shadowy grapefruit-sized colony that would grow into a bulbous, vicious turban if left alone for the rest of the summer. I thought of Ryder, of how this would burn in his belly like a firebrand when he imagined the roughness of another man's hand on my skin.

Billy Ricketts' hand reached my thigh. I was swathed in fear. The beating wings seemed to reach a crescendo, a percussive symphony of intuition without voice. My arm jerked outward, knocking the nest to the floor. Billy Ricketts' fevered hands explored my skin. He did not notice as the nest came alive.

I called out in a solid, extended intonation, "Bees!"

When I was in seventh grade, Billy Ricketts' momma was crowned Corn Queen at the Swagger County fair. While Dovey Ricketts rode down Broad Street on a Fourth of July float, waving to the crowd with an oversized plastic ear of corn in her hand, her son was behind the Daughters of the Confederacy bake sale tent swatting at a yellow jacket who landed on his sticky caramel brownie. Dovey Ricketts would probably have reminded him to sit still and let it finish its business. She might have added that it was more scared of him than he of it. However, she was in a sash and rhinestone crown getting her fifteen minutes, and boys that age never want to sit still.

He probably swatted the yellow jacket away, as most young boys believe themselves to be apex predators over tiny, winged creatures. Likely, he did not realize yellow jackets are predators themselves, social enough to insist you share your sweets, and aggressive enough to fight back when you refuse. Presumably, he did not know yellow jackets, unlike honeybees, can sting, and sting, and sting. Nobody knew, until that Fourth of July as his mother perched atop a float decorated in corn stalks, that he was allergic.

Two days later, the Swagger County Times interviewed her. She thanked God for her crown and the fact that the first aid tent was next door to the bake sale, but we all knew she never forgave her son for the distraction. Nobody remembered the year she was crowned, but everyone remembered the year the youngest Ricketts boy almost died.

There were more words from Billy Ricketts' mouth that I did not care to know. I would not need to know them now. The yellow jackets flew from their nest. He released me, leaped aside. I pressed my back to the wall, standing motionless in the shadows. I watched the windmill of his arms, slapping and swatting. I felt the first sting through the sleeve of Ryder's old green and black plaid shirt.

The pain was smokey and incandescent; however, neither Billy Ricketts nor an insect with a savage instinct to protect its home could do worse to me than what's already been done. I felt a gauzy childhood remnant drop over me, another thing I thought I was out of practice with. For the second time that night, another broken tenet from my youth fit perfectly: no matter how far you think you've grown up from your daddy coming home after drinking away his paycheck, you can still slip back into this. In the blink of an eye, you can disappear from the front lines while you're still standing there.

I felt a sting on my leg like a cigarette stubbed out on

my calf. I connected with the far-off pain through a distant umbilical cord. The violence he brought here in a Cadillac, Ryder coming home, and the yellow jackets felt like they were happening to someone else. I was like a kite, soaring high on an updraft, with no more than a thin, dime-store string to connect my spirit to the motions of my bones and skin far below.

The frenzied hum of insect wings and their agonizing stinging defenses were no worse than the fear I felt as a girl, seeing my daddy's hands balled into fists, red-faced and bellowing, towering over my mother in our kitchen. I'd gone away back then too, and every time, I remembered colors and sounds far more than the brunt of the impact.

I watched Billy Ricketts appear to dance on an electrified floor, an odd calisthenic two-step as he ran past the horses. He rattled the door, agitated and cursing, but the latch stuck. He swatted, frantic, slapping his exposed arms and raking his hands across his face and neck. His face had begun to redden, his lips to swell. He was lucky the nest was small, but not lucky enough. From my orbit, I felt miles away from my thin cotton nightgown, the sensation of his hands on me, the barn.

He clawed at his throat, jerking like a marionette. He wore a mask of fear, something I recognized from my mother, eyes wide, skin blotching red and deeper as the air was forced from her lungs by rough, callused hands. A single yellow jacket hovered near my face, its receptors sucking in and breathing out the pheromones of an all-hands-on-deck emergency to protect their queen. With the slowness reserved for running in a dream, I moved my arm to shield my face. The yellow jacket landed on my sleeve. Searing fire immediately followed, but it was no worse than the echo of a mother's choked voice when her head puts a dent into the drywall in front of her children.

I looked at Billy Ricketts. The yellow jackets had not slowed, darting into the air, circling him, landing and stinging. He came toward me, legs buckling, and sat heavily on a hay bale. His face was fully puffed and doughy. His eyes were almost swollen shut, and his gasps wheezed and squeaked. He slumped to the side and did not brush off a yellow jacket that landed on his forehead. I breathed, allowing one to land on me. I did not move as it crawled up my shoulder, my neck, my cheek. It buzzed away as I closed my eyes. My lashes were not a threat. Now, neither was Billy Ricketts. I came back, snapped back from the ether and into the barn on a rubber band slingshot.

My stings throbbed, raging and frenzied welts I had inflicted on both of us to protect myself and my land, maybe even to save Ryder's life. I walked to the door, now fully present, and felt every bit of the yellow jacket venom. I threw my head back, wanting to scream into the rafters. As I inhaled, I heard the horse whinny, and I knew the animals had witnessed enough chaos. I fought a sob that welled up in my chest and made my eyes prick with tears. Without looking back, I lifted the sticky latch just so and walked up the hill toward the house. I needed to be inside before I could let go. I quickened my pace, focusing on the house. I wanted to sob, to scream, or crumple to my knees in the dark and rip clods of earth from the ground. I did not know what else to do but walk up the hill. My stings had begun to burn and swell, and tears ran down my cheeks.

§

My hands were shaking as I made a paste of baking

soda and water to dab on the welts. I imagined them speaking for me when Ryder came home, "Look what I have done for you, my dearest. I was almost hurt badly in the barn, but I killed a man so he would not kill you."

As I applied the paste, I thought of calling Levi Fisher, the county sheriff. I did not know the law like Billy Ricketts did. I did not know about APBs and roadblocks, but I knew enough to realize I needed Levi.

When the paste was dry, I took the flashlight from the bottom kitchen drawer and did not let the screen door slam behind me as I went down the hill to the Cadillac. A breeze had picked up, carrying my hair over my shoulders. The lightning bugs flashed and twinkled in the field beyond the barn, and the car was a dark hull cramping the drive. I knew Billy Ricketts did not come to my place empty-handed, but I did not know what I was looking for. I shined the flashlight into the car. I had a cartoon flash of a rounded brown sack tied with a string, decorated with a large black dollar sign.

Instead, my beam illuminated a black duffle bag on the floor of the passenger's seat. It was unzipped. The contents were unmistakable. I turned the flashlight off and let my eyes adjust to the darkness. I focused on breathing, trying to think clearly without the bag in my field of vision. My pulse raced. I needed to call Levi Fisher, but I needed to make a decision first. Ryder could come home to, "I killed a man while you were at work," or, "We can pay off the land." I paused. If there was a tally of rights and wrongs for Cadillacs, and barns, and wasps, which side did this duffle bag fall on?

I leaned far into the Cadillac's open window to pull out the bag. It was heavy, and my arms ached from the stings as I carried the bag up the hill with the flashlight off.

The adage about what money can and cannot buy came to mind, but I planned to figure that out for myself. I considered the ways I might tell Ryder about this night. I did not know how to begin, other than, "You remember that Fourth of July parade when Billy Ricketts almost died?"

The Numbers Man

On the second Tuesday in June, a small airplane flew low over the river that bisected Helena, West Virginia into six blocks of downtown and twelve blocks of uptown. A banner with a message printed in large, block lettering trailed the plane.

Downtown traffic slowed at the noise. Drivers pressed against their seatbelts and gazed over the aging two-story brick storefronts. People running errands stepped from the shops onto the cracked sidewalks, five-and-dime merchandise still in their hands. Everyone cocked their heads toward the river. Uptown, people stood in doorways gaping, faces upturned and lunches forgotten. Dogs on sagging porches raised their heads, ears pricked at the unfamiliar droning from above. Helena was far from commercial airline's flight paths, and small planes had few reasons to stray this far into coal country. People craned their necks toward the sky and squinted into the bright blue to make out the banner's words, "The Numbers Man."

Those who shielded their eyes at the wrong moment missed the apparent cloudburst that poured from the plane's underside. It trailed behind the plane for barely a breath. The plume fell, separating into tiny shapes as it descended. Helena's collective eyes, all gazing at the same phenomenon, settled on the drifting, cascading shapes. Was it a flock of miniature, wingless birds? A storm of buoyant hailstones?

Thousands of ping pong balls, each with a black number, fell with a deafening clatter. They ricocheted on the asphalt, the old cars, the leaking rooftops, and on the citizens themselves. Few thought to take shelter. Instead, they froze, engrossed in the spectacle. Balls landed in shopping bags and baby carriages. They bounced into lowered car windows. Shops with doors open to the breeze flooded with balls, and they filled the spaces beneath shelves and racks. The balls covered sidewalks and rolled down the streets in a flash flood of white plastic. The gutters clogged, and the balls piled against car tires like snowdrifts. The citizens were dumbfounded by the cacophony. They scrambled to gather the balls at their feet, unsure of their significance but confident that secrets would be revealed. Someone let out a cry, and they knew The Numbers Man would be there soon.

Lottie Voss did not stand on her porch, starstruck during either grand display. Both times, she was getting ready for work, insulated by the hairdryer and the accompanying bustle that precedes a cocktail shift at the Fortune Hill Casino & Racetrack.

§

Those too young to remember the last visit from The Numbers Man, almost a generation ago, were related to someone who did. Those who remembered it had not been to the event themselves, but they knew someone who had been. Few souls in town did not have a story about The Numbers Man that they could retell with confidence. Each one began with the person who was at the event; their barber's brother, their cousin's fiancé, the third shift foreman who had the job two winters before the mine closed. The third shift foreman told his own story, and it was, in fact, the superintendent who was there.

It was said that those who'd been there and received a ticket with a number, or maybe they selected a ticket from a deep bowl, or perhaps they heard a number read from a ticket and raised their arms with fierce intensity to claim it, received their true number at the event. Those people came away with answered prayers.

The streetcar operator's wife, or was it his sister, had a healthy baby after two stillborns. Some said she already had the baby and it recovered from the measles without consequences. The coat-check girl at Lawson's Department Store, or was it the nurse at Dr. Sharp's office, won the Bingo jackpot at the Protestant Revival Church three weeks in a row. Others remembered her winning the superfecta on the ponies at the new track in Charleston. Helena's populace agreed that there were many truths to be told. When each retelling of the legend offered an incredible bounty, none questioned the lore and its variations.

§

Seasons ago Lottie discovered the racetrack adjacent to the casino had an adoption center for greyhounds past their prime, on long-term losing streaks, or with permanent injuries. Her cheap apartment in a converted Victorian did not allow pets, so she began stopping by occasionally before her shift. Instead of smoking and gossiping about one-night stands and missing child support payments with the other waitresses, she preferred to visit the greyhounds. The years had been far kinder to her than to the other career waitresses her age, and she had little in common with most of them; she did not have a good-for-nothing ex-husband who left her holding the bag, a penchant for shopping or television shows, or nearly grown apples that had not fallen far from the tree.

The dog handlers knew Lottie, expected her to pull a baggie of diced hot dogs out of her purse and ask which dog was up for adoption that week. They did not share in her coddling, however. Greyhounds are working dogs, not pets, living tools used to fill or empty pockets in ninety-second bursts of hope or disappointment. The greyhounds always barked the kennel into a chaos when she entered. When they recognized her and quieted, they were eager to sniff her palm and gobble the meaty chunks she offered.

§

During her freshman year of high school, she bought a Sounds of the Sea disc at a yard sale for a quarter, eventually replacing it with an MP3. The ocean's natural melody in her headphones transported her to a deserted, rocky beach. It was easy to close her eyes and saturate herself with the experience. Soon, she invented a vivid looping vignette and returned to it often. The beach became a place she fit in, unlike the halls of Helena Senior High School. This eased her loneliness when she sat by herself at lunch reading, and when she did not get invited to study groups, parties, or on first dates. Her classmates gossiped about boys, makeup, and senior class football stars. They left their books in their lockers. Lottie read books while walking home, and cared more for the characters than lipsticks or the football stadium on Friday nights. In this way, she felt different and was soon closer to an imagined Atlantic coast than her classmates.

In the vignette fantasy, she is barefoot with her jeans rolled up. The surf crashes against the shore. Calling gulls fly low over the breakers and the dunes. The air is briny and pure, the sun gentle and warm. Clumps of delicate green seaweed dot the shore. She can feel shells and smooth stones beneath her feet in the coarse, pale sand. Seagrasses pepper the dunes.

The wind blows salt spray and her long, fine hair into her face. A dog trots next to her, weaving in and out of the surf. She bends to pick up a piece of driftwood and flings it forward. A dog, a greyhound since discovering the adoption center, races after the stick. The dog forgets the stick for a moment. Ears forward, it bounds through a small flock of brown and white sandpipers hopping on the shore as the waves are sucked toward the sea. The flock takes flight. The dog retrieves the stick and trots toward her with its ears up, and tail held high, proud to have a job.

She envisions the sky a deep blue or steel grey, depending on her mood. Soft, warm waves seem to lap and roll along the shore on blue days. She imagines wading out until she is weightless. On grey days, cold waves roar in her ear and pound a deep bass in her chest. The sea is too turbulent for wading.

The sounds in her headphones and the sanctuary of her daydream were always a reliable escape. She often returned to the rocky shore and the dog with driftwood in its mouth. Listening to the sea became a homecoming, more vivid than a memory. She'd never seen the ocean, but if asked and she answered without thinking, she'd tell of a dog on a beach before she realized she'd never been there.

§

The airplane brought possibilities and unusual hope to Helena, but none knew what to expect. Some said they should bring the gathered ping pong balls to the event. Others insisted they should add up the numbers on their collected balls and present The Numbers Man with sums to divine. A few said the balls were merely fanfare, a grand aerial ticker-tape parade, and they held little significance. They knew they would get a ticket, but to what end? Even amongst the old-timers with vague tales and memories, none knew if there was a lottery drawing, or, tickets be damned, a free-for-all with luck in abundance. It was a comfort to believe in abundance. They stilled their uncertainty at the mystery of tickets, balls, or another method entirely. Instead, they thought about receiving their rightful share. In this way, they were comforted and quite willing to part with their dollars.

Gamblers wanted to tip the casino waitresses and talk about the event in equal proportion. Lottie was happy for both, gushing thanks at the bills, but ambivalent towards The Numbers Man. The gambler's faces, usually slack toward the slot's spinning wheels, became animated and jovial. Each believed they would be the one to convince her. They tipped her well, "Here's a little something so you can save up for your ticket."

The gamblers speculated on buying tickets. When and where would they go on sale? Whatever price The Numbers Man asked was worth it. Some said they'd pay double, but none knew what that amounted to. A few whispered the words second mortgage. Others nodded, knowing they'd put up their house and land for a ticket. The old-timers stated that for those who bought a ticket to the event, The Numbers Man would send the money back like a boomerang. Or he might grant pure luck, and the money and wishes would flow from their taps like water. None had a reason to dispute these theories.

Lottie's face appeared to spring to life with interest every time someone explained what The Numbers Man offered. She stood over them as they sat at the slots, balancing a small, round cocktail tray on her hip, head tilted to the side in feigned attention. In her mind, she tossed driftwood to a greyhound, brushed her hair from her face in the wind, or padded over tiny shells on the warm sand. She inhaled cigarette smoke, served rail whiskey and watery draft beer, and nodded in agreement at how much everyone in Helena needed this.

§

Lottie heard that a vast banner reading, "The Numbers Man," appeared in an empty storefront window next to the True Value Hardware on Market Street. The event's date was hand-lettered in green on a sheet of white paper taped inside the glass. A tall, thin man in wire-rimmed spectacles, thinning pale grey hair, and a black suit stood in the open doorway. He nodded and spoke a few words to someone passing by. They let out a holler. The clerk came out of the True Value, saw the banner and the man, and took her turn at hollering. A line formed at the Market Street storefront that afternoon. The speculation and tall tales of buying a ticket were put to rest. However, there was much rumination as to whether the man in the black suit worked for The Numbers Man, or whether he was The Numbers Man himself. None dared to ask.

The gamblers continued to bet on the dogs and pull the slot arm. Lottie served drinks and emptied ashtrays. She learned who had already bought their ticket in the pay-what-you-wish structure, and who was on their way to Market Street as soon as their machine showed the triple sevens.

§

Lottie listened to the ocean and the gulls in her headphones. She visited the greyhounds. She kept envelopes of cash in a closeted shoebox, adding tips a little faster now that everyone knew The Numbers Man was coming. She learned about what the gamblers wanted: money, new cars and houses, miracle cures, instructions for various something-for-nothing schemes, and assorted ways to return lost and soured love to a lonely heart.

She could not relate to feeling entitled to those things or asking for them because a man with a big reputation was coming to town. There was nobody to answer her prayers or give her the moon, so she was not disappointed by the ordinary things she earned. Helena did not encourage its citizens to chase dreams beyond the county line, so she buried her real wants deep in her belly. She could not share the idea of a future sprinkled with coal dust when she fantasized about salt and sand instead. She forced herself to be satisfied with attainable things and settled into contentment. It was not so bad to set aside a little every month and opt for the luxury of buying books online instead of checking them out from the monthly library van's dated, paltry selection which catered to seniors and housewives.

§

The Numbers Man was four days away.

None would say how much they paid for their ticket from the thin man in the black suit. Allusions to the sum became status symbols. There was little money in Helena for keeping up with the Joneses. However, those who spent the most knew their rewards would outweigh those who spent the least. The most significant benefits would come to those who'd hung their lives in the balance, maybe paying six months of grocery and insulin dollars for a ticket or emptying a savings account when the mortgage was due. Those brave, confident risk-takers, everyone was sure, would garner the best rewards. They agreed that there is little profit in safety. Soon, even the church folks who never spent a dime in the casino gave over to temptation and left themselves broke and hopeful. All risk and carelessness would be forgiven as they took their seats at the event. The anxieties of their deflated bank accounts would be worth it.

§

"Hey there, Mason. Who's up for adoption this week? I brought some jerky." Lottie strode past the handler who was hosing out a small cinder block and chain-link enclosure. She knew small talk was vital so she could continue visiting the greyhounds during non-adoption hours. Mason pointed toward the end of the row. She read the card, "Jane Says Go, unverified record, Florida." The letters TBPD were written across the bottom of the card in red marker. Lottie squatted in front of the enclosure, held out a bit of jerky, and called to the dog. The dog was brindle with mottled black, chestnut, and caramel spots, svelte in the waist with muscled shoulders and a narrow, elegant head and snout.

Mason approached, clearing his smoker's throat. "She's new, just come up from Florida. Sure is a shame."

"What's a shame?" Lottie asked without looking up. Jane Says Go was sniffing at the jerky. Lottie held it through the fencing and Jane Says Go took it without urgency. She leaned her head away to chew and swallow, then pressed her nose through the chain-link. The dog gazed at Lottie, eye to eye. Lottie gazed back. Jane moved her eyebrows and tilted her head, eyes wide, looking directly into Lottie's eyes. Lottie stared. She held the gaze and felt a connection. Jane whined, tilting her head to the other side. Her brows raised again. Lottie's heart filled.

Mason coughed a smoker's cough. "You see the TBPD on the card there? Trainer at the track in Florida must've started bringing her home on the weekends. She got too comfortable and stopped wanting to run. She was up for adoption in Florida for too long, and we're her last chance."

Jane Says Go sniffed Lottie's hand. She reached into her bag for another piece of jerky and fed it to Jane. "Can I open the door?" Lottie asked.

"Might as well. She ain't got but four more days. Go ahead and pet her if you want."

Lottie stood and opened the door. She let Jane sniff her palm again and ran her hand along the length of the dog. She seldom pet the greyhounds, but she was compelled to feel Jane's fur and muscle beneath her palm.

"Thanks, Mason. I've gotta head to work now," Lottie said as she closed the door. She could not get attached to a dog her landlord would not allow her to have. She glanced at him. "What are the letters for?"

"To be put down."

She did not make eye contact with him as she left the kennel. She tried to immerse herself in the coastal loop as she walked toward the casino, but Jane Says Go was more prominent than the ocean. The dog's brindle coat shone in the sun on the shore. She trotted after the driftwood like a companion, not a tool used to fill and empty wallets.

§

Lottie could not stop thinking about Jane Says Go. The waitresses and the gamblers at the slots could not stop talking about The Numbers Man. Many mentioned their ticket's perceived value and what they believed they were entitled to because of it. People she'd known all her life held tickets, some of them substantial when they had hungry children at home and no business laying their cupboards bare. She did not have a long-lost love, a grim medical condition, or a belief that the scales should tip in her favor unless she worked for it. There were no handouts in her world. She could not conceive of the idea that sacrificing the cash in her shoebox meant she would be granted wants she was unsure of. She could not even name a real thing to ask for. She could not adopt a dog. The only other thing she burned for, many hours east of Helena and just beyond the dunes, seemed so far from her grasp that it did not seem possible to ask for.

§

Two decades ago, she made ambitious plans to visit the coast immediately following high school graduation, imagining she would drive to a parking lot that ended in dunes. Her reverie began with the dunes, skipping the drive from Appalachia to the coast. She would park against the dunes, pick her way through the seagrass, and find a dog on a deserted beach. The loop stopped at the dog trotting toward her with driftwood in its mouth. She could not play the scene out much further, so she began it again and again.

Colored with youthful invincibility, she believed she would not get back into her car and drive home to a failing town with a shuttered mine. The Atlantic's gusts would blow Helena's dust from her skin, and she would not wipe off the salt spray that landed on her cheeks. First, she had to leave Helena.

Helena was not as easy to leave as she envisioned. After graduation, there was no money for a road trip or college. The town valued laborers over academics, so she stuffed her disappointment into the place inside her that also held the sea. The Fortune Hill Casino was hiring high school graduates, but it did not offer vacation time for new employees. The idea that she could leave Helena and escape into a place like her ocean daydream became a one-of-these-days idea.

During busy cocktail shifts that left her feeling broken, she imagined walking out of the casino, taking the eastbound interstate, and driving until she could smell the sea. She also pictured the drive to the coast on lonely evenings when the characters in her novels were better company than dates she rarely went on. Although the trip was the only thing she ever set her heart on, the reality of it seemed like winning a jackpot with unpronounceable zeros. Or something from The Numbers Man.

§

Offerings from The Numbers Man seemed to be there for the taking for everyone but her. Why were Helena's laid-off mine workers, cashiers, waitresses, and gamblers more deserving of a fortune? How easy it would be to give in, to bring her shoebox of cash to the ticket booth and sit through an event nobody in town could describe. Why not come away blessed with luck and money like everyone else? She put on her headphones and tried to smell the sea when her mind wandered in this direction. Other times, she imagined bending to stroke Jane Says Go's head as they stood on the shore.

Sometimes, she pictured the unknown of The Numbers Man, then a life with a house of her own in Helena. This was a real thing she could ask for. She imagined endless bookshelves and a job that didn't leave her smelling of cigarettes with sore feet and an aching back. These thoughts left her regretful and wanting, and she always returned to the sea.

§

The Numbers Man was two days away. Lottie did not have a ticket. She began to weigh the closeted box of envelopes against her wants. Her thoughts wound around desires, both essential and frivolous, and few seemed worth The Numbers Man's influence. Her focus on tangible wants in Helena was always broken by gulls sounding over the sea's roar, and the image of herself walking down a beach with Jane Says Go.

She permitted herself one dangerous thought: what would a small ticket hurt? She'd use only her tips from the night before and buy a ticket the day of the event. In this way, Lottie Voss planned to see The Numbers Man.

The permission became anxiety. What if it was a slow night? She considered what she heard about buying a ticket; rather than setting an amount before you got to the Market Street storefront, it was best to take everything you had. You'd tell the man in the black suit what you deserved and coveted and let him help you name your price. When there was nothing in Helena she truly longed for, the thought of this method was an apprehension she could not still with the sounds of the ocean. The ticket and its cost became a small, nervous creature, flexing and growing beneath her sternum.

§

The Numbers Man was one day away.

She dreamed of Jane Says Go the night before. It was a blue-sky day. They walked along the beach as the sun moved across the sky. Mason walked out of the surf with a leash that he clipped to Jane's collar. She could make out the letters TBPD on his tee-shirt. The tide buried her feet in the sand as he led Jane away. She could not follow them.

She had the day off. She decided to buy a ticket with a sacrifice instead of skepticism. This was a snap decision she wanted to own. Three envelopes were three month's rent, a guarantee. She needed only to decide what she wanted to be guaranteed for herself at tomorrow's event. There were years of lonely wants, few friends, and fewer happy romances behind her. A man with the power to fill those holes was one day away. She did not want to let the opportunity pass, so she placed three thick envelopes in her purse after lunch.

§

She wanted to see Jane Says Go before she bought her ticket. She had not come up with anything of value to ask for, but she still had time. The ticket booth was open until no one was left in line. She sat in her car at the kennel, weighing the gravity of her decision. She was in no hurry to part with her money for a grab bag of appetites that did not suit her, so she walked into the building.

Mason was not in the kennel. She walked past the rows of sleek greyhounds until she came to the end. Angry black letters, TBPD, were scrawled on the back of Jane's adoption card. Lottie reached into her purse for a piece of jerky and opened the door. She crouched and held her hand toward Jane. Jane leaped up from the worn plaid blanket she was lying on and bounded over to sniff Lottie's hand. She took the jerky, stretched out her front legs, and pressed her head low to the ground with hips high and tail wagging. She came up, raised her brows, and her eyes widened. She licked Lottie's hand, and Lottie laughed. They contemplated each other.

"Good girl," Lottie whispered, stroking Jane's head. She paused to scratch behind an ear, and Jane narrowed her eyes to relaxed slits. She appeared to smile with the length of her black mouth and leaned into the strokes and scratches.

"What do I want?" was humming inside Lottie like a live power line. She looked into Jane's tawny eyes, took in the brindle speckles as though seeing an animal called a dog for the first time. Lottie inhaled, almost a gasp. She stood up too fast, and her head felt light for a moment. She spun toward the entrance and pulled a leash from the wall.

§

She led Jane Says Go into the grass. Jane sniffed and squatted. Lottie's heart was pounding. Her hands shook. "What do I want?" It was maddeningly simple, yet she'd agonized over the decision. She was willing to sacrifice for the wrong answer, ready to fit herself into a neat box with all of Helena.

Lottie looked down at the greyhound. Half of the answer to her question was a dog named Jane Says Go. The other half was on a rocky beach, just beyond the dunes. She had a GPS and envelopes of cash in her purse and her closet.

Lottie stood in the grass with a sleek dog born to chase driftwood. Jane looked up at her, and Lottie rested her hand on the dog's head. She considered the Market Street storefront, and what it would mean to spend her rent money on a ticket. She considered the letters TBPD and what they would mean for Jane the following morning, many hours before The Numbers Man took the stage. The Numbers Man could not reverse the permanence of angry letters on the back of an adoption card. She contemplated the desires The Numbers Man had fulfilled. None involved second chances. Lottie steered Jane toward the car and knew that for this, a second chance for both of them, she did not need to buy a ticket.

Bird Girl

They were two hours from home. At lunch, she'd suggested an impulse road trip to a small-town bakery with the best chocolate chip cookies in Virginia.

They were walking back to Nash's Blazer, and she squeezed his hand. "Thank you, that was the perfect dessert." He returned the squeeze. She pointed out a statue on the front porch of the rowhouse as they walked past. "What was the name of the book with that statue on the cover? They made it into a movie." Bird Girl was a Savannah icon popular in southern gardens, a short-haired girl in a floor-length dress, holding a shallow bowl in each arm, outstretched and bent at the elbows.

Nash loosened his grip on her hand. Before she could make sense of his actions, he was standing on the porch, bending toward the statue, and turning back to her. Then they ran down the block to the Blazer. Her heart pounded in her chest as she flung open the passenger's side door. She threw herself into the seat and slammed the door shut. She was lightheaded. The Blazer felt like a living creature, filled with the sound of her blood pounding in her ears. Nash's door opened seconds later. He leaped into his seat, hefting the statue past the steering wheel. He slammed his door shut, and the interior came alive with another wave of electricity. He placed the statue on her lap, and she rested her hands on its slender skirt to stop them from shaking. The statue was as long as a squirrel standing on its hind legs, and heavier than it appeared.

"What just happened?" Her voice was breathless and excited.

He turned toward her and winked. "We happened."

"What did you just do? What am I going to do with this?" She looked down at the Bird Girl in her lap and circled her fingers around its waist. She recalled the danger and elation that accompanied leaving a drug store with pockets full of cheap, stolen makeup when she was in junior high. She had not done anything like this as an adult, but the rush she felt was familiar and intoxicating.

He turned to face her. "Put it in your living room." His voice was so confident that she burst into a fit of giggles.

She looked from him to the statue in her lap. "My living room. Good idea." Her apartment was a junior studio fifth-floor walk-up, affordable but small, dark, and cramped. She could not fathom where to put the Bird Girl in such a tiny space. When she moved in, she could not even fit her television once she set up her bookshelves. Regardless of how much she cleaned, the space felt perpetually cluttered.

"It's heavy," she murmured, "and it's not ours." The overwhelming sensation of adrenaline was diminishing into a flutter.

"This street is our street. Those porches are our porches." He motioned toward the rowhouses they were parked in front of. "Twenty feet in every direction belongs to us. We move, the boundary moves, so everything's ours wherever we go as long as we're together." He leaned over the console toward her, and she leaned toward him. She ran a hand over his jaw, brushing her fingers over his sideburns and the stubble along his jawline. Their lips met. His hand cupped the back of her head, and she felt dizzy as the adventure's thrill renewed itself. "As long as we're together," he repeated, lips brushing hers. He pulled away and turned the key in the ignition. She let herself be carried away by his words and the notion that together, they had a power she did not possess when she was alone. It was wondrous to think of the world as theirs, rather than considering that they'd stolen something from someone's front porch.

That night, they lay on their backs on her futon with the lights off and the windows open. He wore boxer briefs, and she wore pale pink cotton underwear. She could not control the heat from the ancient radiators, and the last three days were unseasonably warm for November. She wished she'd shaved her legs that morning. Her apartment felt inadequate; most women her age had mortgages and digital thermostats, instead of cracked plaster walls and heating they could not turn off.

One of his arms was tucked behind his head, and his other hand rested on her belly. They lay without speaking, listening to the shuffled music on her laptop. "You're so beautiful," he said.

"It's too dark in here. You can't even see me." She scooted toward him, and his hand came to rest on her hip.

"I don't need to see you to know how beautiful you are." He raised his palm until only the tips of his fingers were touching her skin. His fingertips moved downwards toward her belly. She felt her skin ripple into goosebumps, and she giggled. "Shh…" he whispered, tracing his fingers over her underwear until he reached the cleft of her closed thighs. She froze, gripped with an old fear that her thighs rubbed too closely together, and her belly was too rounded. He paused and removed his hand. "I'm sorry." His voice was just above a whisper.

"It's okay. I'm okay," she responded, placing his hand on her belly again. He was different than anyone else who'd put his hand on her skin. After a moment, he straightened his fingers until his palm covered her lower belly. His fingers did not stray beneath her lacy elastic waistband, and they were motionless for a moment. She inhaled and put her hand on top of his. It was a signal for "Yes, I want this please," and they each moved closer to the other.

She bent her leg at the knee and felt his hand begin to slide downward. Her hand went slack as his hand moved from beneath hers, and she felt the warmth of his palm between her legs. His fingers straightened, exerting gentle pressure, and her hips rocked to press herself toward him. She matched his strokes with her hips. His body was solid against her, and she leaned into him. She felt his erection on her thigh and reached for it. He grasped her wrist and held it still, whispering, "This is for you." His fingers circled. Her hips thrust. They created a rhythm that became a vortex, and in a sweet and brilliant moment, she tumbled into it with a cry.

She lay next to him, breath ragged and legs twitching, unsure of what to say to break the silence. It was difficult to define her emotions; this was a pathetic time to tell a man she'd been dating for a month that she loved him, but what else could this be? She'd been the first one to use those words far too many times with disastrous results. They had almost become another way to say goodbye because the men she told them to never stuck around to say them back. How else could she define this flood of closeness? She thought about Nash often, and his words from their chocolate chip cookie date echoed in her head: "As long as we're together." Was it too hopeful to imagine that statement held a permanence she could relax into?

Her hand moved toward his belly, but when her fingers moved downward, he stopped her. "We're not doing that tonight. Sometimes it's about you, and sometimes it's about me. Tonight is about you."

She rolled her body toward him and rested her head on his shoulder. If she began thinking about having this, then not having it if she said "I love you" too quickly, it would bring her to tears, so she put it out of her mind. There were a thousand ways to make herself second-guess her actions and regret the things she said. "Let me have this one thing," she thought. She scooted her hips toward him and closed her eyes.

§

The glow of the streetlights through the windshield left the Blazer in thin darkness. "Thank you for dinner," she said, buckling her seatbelt. Nash reached into his coat pocket, then held his hand toward her. His fingers were closed into a loose fist, and she mimicked the gesture, not knowing what it meant. He burrowed his closed fingers into hers until they were wrapped around his fist, then opened them. She felt two small, hard forms sitting on her palm. He lifted his hand and she saw the dainty crystal salt and pepper shakers from the restaurant glinting in the darkness. "You took these?" She was incredulous, but not at the act of dishonesty. Instead, she was enchanted by his thoughtfulness.

The shakers did not fill her with adrenaline like the Bird Girl statue. However, the feeling of power and wonder that overtook her was similar. The act of theft did not occur to her; this small crime took place in a bubble where everything belonged to them as long as they were together.

His grey eyes caught a glimmer from the streetlight. "You said they'd be perfect in your apartment, you know, because of their size."

"I didn't mean... I mean, I love them. Thank you so much." She leaned over the console and kissed his cheek.

He took the shakers from her palm and set them on the dashboard. "We have a thing together. Let me take care of you. I know what you need." He grasped her hand with both of his. "I was looking for you for a long time." She did not know what to say. He released her hand and started the engine. She wedged the shakers into the small pocket in the lining of her purse so they would not spill and thought of the recklessness most of her dates led to. She considered the way she acted on dates with other men, which inevitably left her ashamed and hungover the next morning. She did not feel this with Nash. She had not been left regretful at drinking too much on their first date. He had not even tried to kiss her despite how much she'd drunk. They kissed on their second date, but his hands did not rove further than her waist outside of her coat.

He said they had a thing. A thing could be anything. She wanted one with him, regardless of how undefined it was. He said he'd been looking for her for a long time. It was not impossible to believe she'd also been looking for him. "Thank you," she murmured. She was not sure whether it was a thank you for the gift or something that ran deeper. She could not recall the last person who offered to take care of her or anyone who had done it without speaking the words aloud.

§

She tapped into her phone, "Haircut on my lunch break. See you after work. XO Bird." He began calling her Bird after the Bird Girl statue that took up too much space in her apartment. She liked having a significant nickname, and he had not called her Bridgett since.

His text reply appeared on her screen a moment later. "Skip it. How would you look with longer hair?"

"I don't know. It's been years."

His reply popped up seconds later. "I can wait that long to see it." Her fingers moved in a reflex to reply, but she paused. She did not have a practiced, flirty answer, because she did not know what she wanted to say. What were the right words to tell a man she would skip a haircut because he asked her to? Would she have done this for any of her other relationships? Her hair was jaw-length, a crisp classic bob she'd worn for years. It was almost her signature. She smiled into her screen as another text appeared. "I'm ordering you a salad delivery for lunch. Balsamic vinaigrette, right?"

"You remembered! You don't have to do that." She tapped a smiling emoji with hearts for eyes and tapped her nails along the back of her phone. She wanted to press her hands into his. She wanted her touch to communicate something more meaningful than, "Thank you for being this way with me."

"I'm stopping you from driving to the salon. See you tonight." A moment later, another text appeared. "Wear your black sweater. Got to get back to work now."

She tapped a response, "Can't wait to see you tonight." She waited for his reply, but her screen was silent.

§

"I don't know how you feel about celebrating little things," he said.

She leaned toward him and murmured, "I like celebrations." They were sitting close together on her futon, thighs touching. His arm was draped over the back of the futon, and her shoulder was tucked against his ribs. They were splitting a bottle of her favorite Chardonnay. He drank more slowly than she did and never ordered white wine when they went out. "You don't really like white wine, do you?"

"I'll have what you're having." His face broke into a smile, and she giggled. "I always wanted to say that."

"Oh my God, Nash. You don't have to keep drinking this. I have a bottle of red in the cabinet. I'm so sorry I never asked." She moved to untangle herself from the futon, but he wrapped his arm around her shoulders.

"I want to taste what you taste when we're together." His grip on her shoulders tightened, and he pulled her toward him. "Did you realize tonight's the six-week anniversary of our first date?" Her heart fluttered in her chest, and she thought of the butterflies that everyone talks about. The kind of man who gives you butterflies does exist, she mused, thinking of her best friend Alicia's statement that people made up butterflies for love songs and bad poetry.

"I didn't realize that. I didn't know you were counting." She felt inadequate. They'd gone out for margaritas on their one-month anniversary, and she was looking forward to month two, but she didn't think to count weeks.

"I got you something. It's not a real present, but I was thinking about you." He leaned away from her to reach into his messenger bag on the floor beside him. "Close your eyes," he said, turning toward her. She closed them. He did not say anything, and she sat still with closed eyes. "Open your mouth," he said.

"What do you have?" She opened her eyes and giggled.

"Close your eyes," he snapped. Her eyes closed, and her hand instinctively flew to her mouth. She pressed her fingers to her lips, uncertain and startled. He did not speak for a moment, and she did not move. "Open your mouth." His tone was soft again, and she dropped her hand to her lap. Her lips parted, and he said, "Wider." She hesitated, wondering what he'd retrieved from his bag. "Wider," he repeated. She obeyed. Her heartbeat quickened. The room was silent. She could not even hear him breathing as she sat next to him with eyes closed and mouth gaping. "Okay," he said.

She opened her eyes and blinked into his face. He was not holding food toward her. In fact, his hands were empty. "What was that about?"

"Trust, Bird. I need you to trust me."

"I do trust you, Nash. I just didn't know what you were going to do."

"Trust is when you do things without asking why. I know you trust me, Bird Girl. I just want you to trust me one hundred percent. We can get there." She looked at her hands in her lap. Had she disappointed him on their six-week anniversary? She did not know this was an occasion or that there would be a test. Would he still give her the present if he didn't think she trusted him? "I thought about you when I went to upgrade my phone a few days ago. Yours has that crack on the screen, and I wanted to do something nice for you." He reached beneath his leg and held a phone toward her.

"This phone is practically new. I can't take it from you." She glanced at her phone in the Bird Girl statue's bowl. He was right about the crack, but it was outside of her budget to do more than limp along until it was time for an upgrade in eighteen months.

He pressed the phone into her hand. "I kept it on my plan. You can use it for a Wi-Fi hotspot, so I want you to cancel your cell phone and internet service." She turned her body toward him and nestled closer, circling her arms around his shoulders. She thought of the bills she struggled to pay every month, and how this would ease her burden. Her lips met his earlobe, and she whispered too many thank yous in his ear.

He leaned back and looked into her eyes. "You don't have to thank me. I just want you close to me."

She straightened and looked away from him. "I'm so sorry."

"Sorry for what?" His voice was amused, but he did not laugh. She sensed that he already knew what she was going to say.

"That opening my mouth thing. I didn't trust you enough. Now you've given me a new phone, and you're paying my bills." Her voice cracked, and she felt her throat tighten. "I trust you. I trust you so much."

"We'll get there, my girl. I'm the only one you can really trust." He pulled her into him and guided her head onto his shoulder. He ran his hand over her head and neck, almost petting her, and she felt his shoulder beneath her cheek grow warm and damp with her tears. She was starting to worry that the words, "I love you" would erupt from her mouth without her consent. He was so kind to her, yet she failed to show him she trusted him. It was difficult to feel worthy of a man like this who had so much to offer. What did she have to offer in return, aside from herself? Somehow, that did not feel like enough.

"Can you stay over tonight?" She thought back to the

night he said it was all about her. Tonight, it would be about him.

"I have an early meeting tomorrow. I can't stay, but I'd like to hold you until you fall asleep." They stood up, and each took an edge of the futon. They unfolded it in unison, and she spread the blankets over it. "I'll be right back," she said, thinking of the lingerie she wanted to wear to bed. Her wardrobe had so few flattering nightclothes. However, she recently ordered an expensive matching set of three short nightgowns in different animal prints. The model appeared confident and sexy, and she hoped Nash would see her that way while she was wearing them.

"Take your time," he called after her as she walked toward her dresser to retrieve the leopard-printed one.

§

Bird set a shopping bag at Alicia's feet and sat next to her on the futon. It was good to see her best friend after so many weeks. "I missed you," Bird said, leaning over to embrace her friend.

"Me too, Bridgett. How's your new boyfriend? You're hardly around anymore."

"He's great. Really great. I think he's the one." She motioned toward the bag, and Alicia reached into it. "It's all yours if you want it," Bird said.

"You sent me a picture of these right after you ordered them. What happened?" Alicia held up a short, zebra-striped nightgown with a ruffle at the hip. "This one's pretty cute."

"They just didn't work out." Bird grasped the ruffle and rubbed her fingers together over the stretchy, nylon material. "Nash doesn't like the way they feel."

"Nash? Since when do you give brand-new things away because of a boyfriend?" Alicia's hands dropped and the nightie fell into a pile on her lap. She rolled her eyes and repeated Bird's words in a mocking tone, "Nash doesn't liiike them."

"Stop," Bird giggled. "I got them for him, and he doesn't like them. What am I going to do with them if I can't wear them?"

"You can wear them," Alicia responded, stressing the word *can*. "Don't let a new man start telling you what you can and can't do. Is that what this whole bag is about?" She pointed at the shopping bag on the floor at her feet. Bird looked at the bag, then back at Alicia.

"This whole bag," Bird began, "is full of things I don't wear anymore. Let's be glad we're the same size, or I'd have to give them to my aunt." Both women laughed, thinking of Bird's aunt's compulsive shopping habits and her closets and drawers filled to overflowing.

Alicia was perpetually involved in short-lived, disappointing flings with men who wouldn't be anyone's Mister Right. They'd supported each other for years through disastrous first dates and breakups and used cheap wine and chocolates to ease each other's pain. In all the years they'd known each other, Bird could not recall her friend ever dating a man like Nash, or wanting to please a boyfriend in any way.

Alicia reached into the bag and retrieved a silky, pink blouse with a plunging neckline. "I used to love that one," Bird murmured.

Alicia pulled a pastel yellow Angora sweater with a deep V-neck out of the bag. "Too much cleavage in these?"

"It's just not me anymore."

Next, Alicia held up a pair of black, strappy heels.

"What's wrong with these?" She eyed the straps, then turned one shoe over to examine the sole. "These are new. How are they something you don't wear anymore? Wait, Nash again? He doesn't like the way your toes look?"

"I forgot that other bag of shoes in the closet. It's not my toes, it's just that he likes me in flats."

Alicia snorted and tossed the shoes onto Bird's lap. "Let me guess, you let Nash go through your closet. You kept all your Little House on the Prairie dresses, and I got the rest."

Bird tossed the shoes back to Alicia and shook her head. Her tone was serious. "You have no idea. He's the best man I've ever been with. At my age..." She paused for a moment. "Why would I keep wearing things he doesn't like? I have plenty of other things to wear. I don't care that much about these things anyway."

"You know what? I wasn't going to bring this up, but I have your entire wardrobe on my lap because of some boyfriend I hardly know. I could tell there was something off that time I met him." Bird began to speak, but Alicia continued. "We don't go get pedicures anymore. You changed your number, and you don't even have to do that when you get a new phone. You're growing out your hair, and I know how much you hate hair on your neck. And a padlock around your wrist? My God, Bridgett—"

"You don't understand," Bird interrupted. "You don't know what a relationship is like when someone cares about you and wants to take care of you. You can't even comprehend what we have together."

"I can comprehend things pretty well. This is about controlling you, not taking care of you. I don't know what else this is. I haven't seen you in weeks, so I called your aunt. She hasn't heard from you either, and she's also wondering what's going on with you." Alicia shook the strappy high heel toward Bird. "None of this makes sense. You hate flats."

Bird felt her stomach tighten as she remembered Nash's assessment of her friend. He said Alicia was bitter and envious of what they had. He honed in on her inability to maintain a relationship and said she would never tolerate Bird finding happiness first. Bird saw that he was right. A true friend would be happy for her. She sighed and looked at Alicia, who was sitting silently, holding a shoe.

"I've got to get going." Alicia stood, dropped the shoes into the shopping bag, and looped the handles over her forearm. Bird stood, gathered the Angora sweater and the pink blouse, and tucked them into the bag on top of the shoes. Both women were still for a moment. They'd never needed the skills necessary to resolve spats, and neither knew what to say. "Thank you for the bag," Alicia said, turning toward the door. In three strides, her hand was on the knob. She paused and looked back at Bird.

"I'm sorry," Bird said in a meek voice.

Alicia exhaled through her nose. "Have fun with Nash. I'll tell your aunt you're alive and well." She turned the knob, stepped through the door, and closed it behind her without saying goodbye. The apartment was silent. Bird did not move for a few moments. She reached for her phone, resting in one of the bowls the Bird Girl statue held in her outstretched arms. Her first impulse was to tell someone about the spat. Before Nash, she'd have called Alicia and her aunt about any dramatic situation and discussed the details with whoever answered first. She set the phone back in the bowl. Neither were people she could confide in anymore.

He was right about her aunt, a critical, bitter spinster

who guilted her into doing favors. She had nothing to offer in return but more guilt for not being good enough. She left her aunt's townhouse wracked with anxiety more often than not but kept going back because her aunt was her only family. Nash had pointed this out and given her countless other reproachful examples she had been blind to on her own, and he'd helped her finally cut ties. She was happier for her efforts and grateful to Nash for seeing what she could not. Something similar happened with Alicia. It was now clear that her best friend wanted to keep her in the cycle of bad first dates that Alicia could not break. She wondered how Nash could have so accurately analyzed her family and friends in ways that had always eluded her.

She looked at the small, sterling silver padlock on an elegant, linked silver chain around her wrist. Alicia should have been happy for her, but instead, she sneered at the bracelet. Nash presented it to her on their two-month anniversary, shortly after the three words she was afraid of had escaped her lips. He repeated them back to her and added that he'd been waiting to make sure she knew he was the one. He said her words gave him the permission he needed to make her his. Her fingers circled her wrist over the chain, and she squeezed them closed, feeling the links pressing into her skin. Nash had done this after he clasped the lock around her wrist. His fingers were far more powerful than hers, and she'd winced at the pressure.

"A ring comes off," he said. "This doesn't." His eyes locked with hers and he pulled her close, fingers still circled around her wrist. "You're locked to me with this."

He wanted her locked to him. She tried to remember the rest of his words, but the way she felt was a more prominent memory. The feeling of belonging to someone who actually wanted her there was unfamiliar and overwhelming. Her heart swelled at the memory. She looked at the door and thought of Alicia walking out in frustration and jealousy. "I deserve someone like him. I deserve this," she said aloud to the seat on the futon that Alicia no longer occupied.

§

"Can I please have a small skim vanilla latte, and a chicken salad on wheat to go?" Bird handed a gift card to the cashier.

"I love this one. It was a limited-edition design," the cashier responded as she swiped the card.

"Thank you. My boyfriend gave it to me."

"He's a good one." The cashier handed the card back, and Bird moved away from the register to wait for her order. Her mouth twisted into a smirk as she leaned against a high-backed bar stool next to a woman working on her laptop. A cashier in a chain coffee shop could see that Nash was a good one, but her own best friend could not.

He'd been right about Alicia and about her family. He'd also been right about her only male friend, Darren, pointing out that he'd make a move on her sooner or later. Why else would Darren have hung out at her apartment during the times she was single, then patiently waited out every doomed relationship? Why would he have opened doors for her, listened to her breakup woes, and refused to let her pay when they went out for drinks? Darren was a shoulder to cry on for years. He never made an advance on her, regardless of how much she had to drink. Something clicked in Bird's mind when Nash pointed out that Darren was simply waiting for the right time. Realizing this, she could not maintain their friendship.

“Small vanilla latte,” the barista called out, setting her drink on the counter. She picked it up and moved back to the bar so she could send a text.

“Just got a latte. Thx for the card,” she tapped into her phone.

A moment later, Nash’s reply flashed across her screen. “I know. Corner of King and South Union. Enjoy.”

“Are you following me?” She added a winking emoji and tapped send.

“Don’t worry about that.” A smiling emoji with tiny devil horns appeared below his words. She loved this game. Sometimes he said he had people following her. Other times he alluded to following her himself. She was a creature of habit. Her routines took her to the same places on the same days of the week, and Nash’s words about having her followed meant only one thing; he paid enough attention to her to remember her patterns. She knew she was not being followed. However, how bad would it be to have someone care for you enough to want to consume every move you made? If Darren said these things to her, she’d be uncomfortable. It felt natural for Nash to go one step further, to cross a line that Alicia and her aunt would have balked at. “They don’t understand. They’ve never had this, but they’d kill for it if they had a taste of it,” she thought and took a sip of her latte.

Once again, Nash’s presence created overwhelming emotions, and she had to take a pause. Her peers were finding laugh lines and watching their children grow into young adults. Instead of those things, she was discovering the first thing in her life that had ever felt real. It was warm and safe, with Nash’s arms like a cocoon she could climb into and be free of the world’s dangers.

She sipped her latte and considered how proud she

was of herself for articulating the single, boundless trait that drew her to him. In other relationships, she'd been accused of being clingy and smothering. Nash seemed to welcome it, and she could trace her feelings to a wellspring that sometimes caused her eyes to fill with tears of gratitude.

For every embrace, every fingertip drawn over bare skin, and every whispered phrase of pillow talk, Nash had one of his own for her. She could tell him she was his a dozen times in a dozen ways in one evening. Every time, he'd pull her close and repeat the sentiments to her without tiring. Every gesture of affection was received and reciprocated with equal enthusiasm, not rebuffed for being needy. Inside her was a bottomless well of want, wanting to love and be loved in return. She recognized this feeling in him, and it felt charmed to have found an equal partner to share her love with. There was no other explanation for how he asked so much of her and offered so much of himself in return.

She looked at his last text on the screen and responded with a single red heart. She scrolled through the view of sent messages to others and noticed how long it had been since she responded to a text other than Nash's. Her aunt offered nothing more than guilt and anxiety. She had no friends other than Alicia and Darren, and Nash was right about both of them. She'd been blind to who she kept company with. There was no reason to maintain relationships with people who did not want the best for her.

"Chicken salad on wheat to go." She looked up to see a sandwich wrapped in red and white striped paper sitting on the counter. The sandwich maker gave her a slight wave before turning toward the next sandwich order on his list.

§

Forty was a milestone birthday, an age her college self would have thought of as over the hill. Instead, the last year felt like a triumph. The year ahead and those to follow seemed to sparkle in her future. She laid out two pairs of earrings on the counter and held one from each pair up to her lobes. She never wore dangling earrings when her hair was short, and she enjoyed the novelty of both her long hair and the jewelry Nash bought her. His master bath had so much more counter space than the tiny sink in the crowded studio apartment she used to live in. Her makeup, toothbrush, and a small, ceramic frog were tucked into a small drawer next to the sink, and she admired the vast, empty white marble surface of the vanity. She knew Nash wouldn't ask her to get rid of the frog, a souvenir from a spring break vacation to Florida with Alicia, but it didn't hurt to keep it out of sight.

She settled on an earring, and then held it next to the chain around her neck. It was a twin in style and meaning to the padlock bracelet he'd given her on their two-month anniversary. It was hard to remember herself not wearing the matching set every day. Her life felt dark back then when she'd been careening through the world without thinking or having anyone on her side. She looked at the delicate silver hoop earring in her hand, then at the bracelet, and felt relieved at the milestone. She could not have conjured up a more perfect way to begin this decade of her life than if she asked Nash to design something special for her.

He was in the kitchen preparing her birthday dinner, and she knew not to enter when he was busy. She had a moment of nostalgia for old birthdays spent with Alicia and Darren at a neighborhood bar they could walk to from her apartment. Every year, they'd drink too much and lament being unmarried and working dead-end jobs at their ages. In those days, there were no padlocks. Her old office job barely covered her expenses. The parade of disappointing relationships felt endless. She realized her feelings were bittersweet, not nostalgic.

Her phone rang and brought her out of the reverie. She snatched it from the counter and silenced the ringer without looking at the screen. She knew the caller would begin with three words, "Happy birthday, Bridgett." On every birthday before Nash, she'd been a person she did not like and wanted to forget. He helped her change things in such dramatic ways that she could not even identify with being called Bridgett. She sat on the bed and sunk into the plush, down comforter, tucking her phone beneath her pillow to remove the temptation to look at it. Whoever it was could wait.

"Bird girl, come down," Nash called from the bottom of the stairs. She had forgotten to put on her earrings but did not want to keep him waiting. As long as she was wearing her bracelet and necklace, other jewelry did not matter. She bounded down the steps toward him. "Come into the living room before we eat," he said, taking her hand. They laced their fingers and walked to the couch together. He motioned for her to sit, but he did not sit next to her. The couch's black leather was cool beneath her thighs. The sleek, spare lines of Nash's birch and black leather Danish modern decor always felt aloof to her, and she dug her bare toes into the carpet's deep pile for a bit of comfort.

"What are we doing?" Bird knew how long he'd been in the kitchen preparing dinner, and they rarely ate in the living room.

"I decided not to wait until after dinner for your present."

"Do I have to close my eyes for it?" she asked, referring to the first time he'd given her a present and asked her to trust him. As their relationship progressed, closing her eyes or performing other small, innocuous tasks became less about uncertainty and more about proof that she trusted him. She was proud that she had not failed any of his small tests in many months.

"Close your eyes, but just for a moment." She closed her eyes like a reflex. Her fingers did not fly to her lips, and her shoulders did not tense. "This is different," he said. She heard his shoes walking over the polished wood floor into the kitchen. He paused for a beat, and his footsteps were calculated as he returned. She knew not to open her eyes as he set something on the cushion next to her. He did not speak. She did not move. She was accustomed to this. Something rustled next to her, and she could sense his presence inches from herself.

"Okay," he said, and her lap came alive, warm and wiggling. A black kitten with large, golden eyes was staring up at her.

"A kitten, thank you!" She cradled it in her arms and nuzzled its soft, fine fur against her cheek. It purred deeply. Her eyes welled with gratitude. Here was a friend to spend time with during Nash's long workdays. When she was tired of reading, there were only so many exercise videos and cooking shows that she could tolerate. "A kitten," she repeated into its fur. The kitten reached a paw toward the padlock dangling from her wrist. It was mesmerized by the shiny trinket. She watched it extend a paw to swat at the tantalizing charm.

She saw its small, translucent claws extend as it made contact with the padlock, barely missing catching one in the miniature keyhole. She looked at the keyhole for a moment and realized she'd never thought to ask for the key.

Black Dog

I hear the words "four years." I realize I have been holding my breath. Otherwise, I might have gasped. The judge does not bang a gavel. There would have been a solace in the sound, a punctuation mark of finality. My throat tightens and I feel my eyes begin to prick with tears. The words have made my mind foggy. I lock eyes with Carter across the courtroom. My lips know they should be moving; we could be a scene in a movie with my mouth forming into meaningful last words he will take with him. Instead, my lips part, mute and still. My brow knits. His eyes are narrowed, lips pressed into a thin, pale slash. I imagine the pressure of his jaw, molars crushing into each other to keep him silent. I am also silent in my hard wooden courtroom seat.

Our eyes hold on to each other, an embrace we have not been permitted. I watch as the bailiff, dull brown uniform and heavy belt of rural Virginia justice, places a hand on Carter's shoulder. He stands, holding my eyes, and allows himself to be led away. I close my mouth. My lips do not know the shapes that would make a response to the judge's words, or a goodbye. I cannot quantify this with language. I sit still in my seat. If I leave, I leave Carter. The room is emptying. It is difficult to put a measure of understanding on that many days.

I think of the calendar on the kitchen wall from the feed supply store in town. After dinner, I will draw a red X on today's square. In four years, I will not remember today's X. I do not know how else to put the judge's words into something I can hold in my hand. I will tell the dog about the X. She will stand beside me as I draw it. I will tell her we are one day closer to Carter's coming home day.

§

Glory laps the gravy from her bowl. I watch red rosebuds appear beneath her tongue on the china, my grandmother's wedding set. I still cook for two with Carter gone, but Glory does not take Carter's chair across from me. I thought to feed her at the table in the beginning. The worn, high-backed wooden chair, Carter's domain, does not suit her. The seat is too small for a dog of her size. She is my closest friend, but she will not claim his place. She has taken well to her new diet, the same as mine now because I do not like to cook for one. She is not a picky eater.

I place my plate on the heart pine floor, and she laps at the gravy. I moved the old everyday dishes to the top cupboard shelf. The passed-down wedding set for company and holidays serves a better purpose. It used to mean there was a special occasion, a thing that would come and go. It still means this, but that thing is measured in seasons now. I mark a red X to measure that thing, and the wedding set says it will be over. I need things to tell me that. On Carter's coming home day, we will go back to the everyday set. The passed-down set will go back to waiting for the next occasion that will come and go.

Glory sits next to my chair, eyes fixed on my face. I stroke her head. She is a mutt, soft and black with expressive brown eyes that look bronzed in the sun. She is waiting for me to say, "Let's go." We have turned each other into creatures of habit; she knows it is almost time to go outside. I place the dishes in the sink and run the tap over them. It is not necessary. She does not leave food on our plates.

The tap has started dripping again. I think of pliers, washers, how far to get on my own before I have to call a man out. I have learned that I can silence a squeaking hinge and replace a fuse in the cellar. It does not take much either to stop a running toilet. I try to keep up the old place well enough, but it is needy. The third stair's groaning creak is louder. The paint on the porch is chipping. The crack in the living room windowpane seems longer every time I look at it. I fill the space in a room differently now, no longer a feminine presence to work alongside the maleness of my husband. After Carter left, I set aside everything about myself that was once easy on the eyes. When my husband returns and my hair has grown back, I will become a wife again.

Now, my work is to tend our two acres, and Glory and the hogs. I believe this is what Carter sees in his mind like a snapshot of comfort. I call to Glory. We stand before the calendar, an unadorned shrine. She knows to sit when I look down at her. I draw the X and look at her again. I say Carter's name aloud the way you would teach a child to speak. I have no other way to keep him fresh in her mind. Last year's calendar hangs on the nail behind this year's version. I could not bring myself to get rid of the catalog of days. I will need a longer nail when I am nearer to the last X than I am today.

During the first calendar, I wished for more than an X and Carter's spoken name. Glory and I stood silent before it for long moments when I wanted grand actions but did not have them. I cannot say whether the X is happy or sad. The Xs already there means his coming home day is closer, but the blank spaces mean I have to fill them up. I don't try to make more of it now. The wedding china helps. My hair, cut off to my chin the day I left him in the courthouse, helps as well. Every day it grows imperceptibly, another thing like special-occasion dishes that will be righted when I have filled enough calendars. The X is made. Glory stands. I cap the marker and reach for her leash.

§

The land across the road is vast and wild. It has been for sale and untamed for so long that the handwritten numbers on the For Sale sign are missing curls and angles. It would take a few tries on the phone if you guessed wrong that an eight was a three or six. There is no street number. You would have to say it was the place on Furnace Road with the wooden, slat-rail fence. If there was once a No Trespassing sign, I do not remember it. Glory and I cross the road and walk past the rotting fence. She trots to sniff at the base of a broad, gray rock protruding from the weeds. I lean against its cool surface, running my hand over a pillow of moss. It would take so much to love this land enough to buy it. Who would want the work of leveling the hillocks and crushing the boulders to make it a home? It is a better place for us to walk the rutted dirt track while Glory catches scents of small, elusive prey.

A breeze blows toward us. Glory looks away from the stone and points her head into the breeze. Her lids narrow in concentration. Her mouth opens, lips and nose flexing as though tasting the scent. We have learned to pause together on our walks, each trying to sense what has captivated the other. I inhale through my nose, but the allure is lost on me. The gust softens. She looks toward me, asking if I'm ready to continue. If I do not move, I can hold us here for many moments. Her glance will dart around. She will listen, concentrating, seeking out a reason for my stillness. If she does not move, she can do the same to me. I will pause and try to determine what has grasped her attention. She is more attuned to what I cannot perceive and likely to know what I'm looking at before I know it myself.

We walk on the primitive dirt track, hardly a road anymore. Tufts of pale grasses grow knee-high on either side. Sometimes along this road, I talk to Glory about Carter in a loud voice. I do not want to creep up on something wild she would be eager to investigate. These words are how I keep him alive for both of us. She presses her nose into things I would not care to smell. Sometimes she sniffs too closely, or paws at the earth. These times, I move her along. My voice takes on Carter's tone when I deliver commands; "leave it," or "drop it." She is a good girl, and it is rare that I have to ask her twice. Carter could not have known his hours spent training her would be for me more than him. She does not pull on the leash. Sometimes I match her pace when the urgency of her nose quickens her step. Other times, I say, "Walk with me." She walks by my side, looking up at me when I call out to let the creatures know they are not alone.

The end of this hard-packed dirt path fades from red clay into tall grasses and weeds. There is not even a stone foundation or crumbling chimney nearby. We cannot see Furnace Road or our house from here. This is where we turn around, and she sniffs the grass on the other side of the track. She watches a brown moth fly from a knot of flowering weeds she has pressed her nose into. The land is still and quiet, and it is cooling with the first hints of fall. The sun sets into the golden hour. Glory's black fur gleams and her eyes catch the light. I can see the age-old wolves in her blood.

A dull, red pickup truck is parked just inside the fence. The fence extends for the length of the property, and we must walk past it to get home. I do not recognize this truck. I grasp Glory's leash close to her collar, and she matches my pace, head at my hip, ears straight. Our steps become strides. Her stance is the thing I would do if rising to my full height was meaningful. I stand as tall as men's noses, chins, or shoulders, but a woman with Glory at her side does not need to be large. A man is walking toward the truck from the fence line. He waves. I raise my arm in return. I am not afraid of this stranger, but I am wary. Glory is also suspicious as he approaches. We stop just outside the fence as the man begins to speak.

"Hello, ma'am. Is this your property?" The man's face is lined and tan. He is slight, and so slender that my hips may be wider than his. The ends of his mustache extend toward his chin, but he does not have a beard. His salt and pepper hair, parted in the middle, brushes his shoulders. He would not look out of place with a vintage steel guitar.

"No, this isn't our place. We're just out on a walk." Glory is still, staring at the man who has fixed his gaze on her.

"Some dog you got there," he says to her without looking at me. "A black dog." She is motionless, head and ears pressing forward. I do not like his tone. Glory is not a threat unless called to be.

"You're right," I respond. I rise to my full height through her presence again. It is rare for me to be alone with strangers without her. I remember a time before her when my hands would have shaken during this encounter. Now, they are still. My response agrees with him that she is big. Her response, black fur and the stillness of attention, agrees with him as well.

"Well, I aim to buy this place, ma'am. My name's Pastor Ronnie Dixon. Pleased to meet you." He nods, raising his hand into a wave again. I am grateful that we are standing too far apart for a handshake. It appears that he is changing the subject from Glory on purpose.

"I'm Bree." I am struck by the idea of someone wanting to own this land. "Do you have people around here?"

"I come over from Tennessee. I got in my truck and started driving. I knew I'd know where I was going when I got there. When I saw the For Sale sign on the fence, I knew the Lord had led me here."

I relax my grip on the leash. I stroke Glory's head. It is not neighborly to keep a dog of her size at attention. Glory does not run free, and our new neighbor is not required to like dogs.

"You live nearby?"

"My husband and I live across the road." I glance toward home. The sun will be setting soon, and I have not left a light on. A husband would turn the lights on if he were home. I do not want to walk into a darkened house with a stranger nearby. "It was nice to meet you, Pastor Dixon. It's time for us to be getting on in." I flex my wrist to tug at Glory's leash. She looks up at me. I take a step into the road, and she follows. "This is Glory, by the way."

"A dog," he responds. "Right across the road." He looks at her in the way of a man sizing up another who is broader than himself. It could be that he is fearful of dogs. I nod my head and turn away. Neither of us says goodbye as Glory leads me home.

§

Glory and I feed the hogs after breakfast. They were breeding hogs before our closest neighbor died a month after Carter left. His wife spoke of taking them to auction. Two days earlier, I'd been in our small, empty barn planning for chickens and a coop I'd have to build. Instead, I repaired the pen and added a shelter to the adjacent outdoor run. A few days later, I was repeating their names, Ginny and Maggie, the way I say Carter's name to Glory. To the neighbor, they were vacant creatures that brought piglets and dollars to his farm. I first thought to stop them breeding and turn them into friends. They respond only to my shrill calls of "Here, pig-pig, su-su-su," at feeding time. I cannot win them over. It is enough to know these old girls can rest on my land, well-fed, and no longer breeding. They are both large and solid. I am surprised at how much they eat, but it is nice to have company in the barn.

Glory and I cross the road. We pass the fence and the faded For Sale sign. Glory sniffs and trots. I am lost in my thoughts: splitting wood for the woodstove, going into town, the crooked front gate we rarely use but should still be set straight. I notice tire tracks on parts of the road that are not overgrown. I think of Pastor Dixon's small truck bumping along the ruts, exploring the land he has been drawn to. I am drawn here for its wildness, not for its potential. There is a sense of something bigger than myself when Glory and I cannot see Furnace Road, and the only sounds are what nature has placed beyond the rotting, wooden fence.

A towering, white cross has been erected at the end of the road. It is freshly painted and set into a circle of concrete. I run my fingers along the cross's rough surface. The stark white newness is too much of a contrast to this land's feral character. I am uneasy standing before a testimony that our aloneness on this land has ended. I look down at Glory. She is sniffing the intrusion, nose pressed close to the ground near the concrete. I step away from the cross. "Come," I say to Glory, but it is not necessary. She looks at me. Her ears are forward. Her tail is erect. She is attuned to my movements and knows it is time to leave.

§

"Hello there." I look up and lean the shovel against the hog pen. Pastor Dixon is standing in the doorway with his hand raised in a wave. He lowers it as I turn to face him. "I came over to say hello and meet your husband. Is your dog put up?"

I have been mucking out the pen, and my hands are filthy. I use the crook of my arm to wipe the sweat from my forehead. He does not know how badly I want to say my husband is home, and then call out to Carter. "My husband went into town, and Glory's in the house," I respond. He looks over his shoulder toward the house as though Glory is listening. I grasp the shovel and step out of the pen. "I was just finishing up in here." I carry the shovel toward the door, the barn's only exit. I do not want to be in the barn, while Glory is inside the house and Carter is many miles away.

We stand in the dirt yard facing each other. I hold the shovel as I would hold Glory's leash. I want something to do with my hands while I consider ways to say my husband is not home but will be soon.

"How many animals you got in there?" He looks past me into the barn.

"Just the hogs," I respond. The barn is not large, and it is evident that we do not have a pasture for horses. "Do you have animals?" I can find things to say about animals until dinnertime if it will keep him from asking about Carter again.

"Nice place." I notice he has ignored my question. "You been here long?" He turns away from me, looking at the field and tree line beyond the barn. Before I can respond, he asks, "How much land you got? You own the woods back there, too?"

I turn the corners of my mouth up into a smile that does not reach my eyes. "Are you looking to move in with us," I ask with sarcasm. I am uncomfortable being peppered with questions, but at least they are not about meeting my husband.

He lowers his voice. His casual air disappears. "You already know what's on my land. I got a right to know the same about you." This does not feel like a new neighbor dropping by to say hello.

I smile cordially to break the tension. "Thank you for stopping by, Pastor Dixon. I'm sorry you missed my husband." I do not want to give him the chance to bring the conversation around to meeting Carter. Pastor Dixon matches my pace as I begin walking away from the barn. It is time for him to leave, and I want him to know that. It will be challenging to keep up with the story that Carter is here, but not here right now. We stop at the end of the driveway next to the mailbox and I try to sound pleasant. "I've got to get the hogs fed and get dinner on."

He turns toward the land that still bears a faded For Sale sign on the fence. "You have a good evening, neighbor."

§

I continue to mark a red X on the calendar and say Carter's name aloud every night. I try not to think of filling two more calendars with red Xs. I think, instead, of the full day's drive I will take soon, and the one I will take every month for the next two years. I picture Carter behind smudged, scratched glass, pressing a phone to his ear. I will hold a phone to my ear as well. I do not try to predict the words we will speak. I want the image of his face to fill my mind. It is still as clear as fifteen years' worth of photographs of us on our wall, or on my phone. Mostly, I want to sit before him, wrap my eyes around him, and freshen the memories I will take home with me.

I feed the girls, calling out, "Here, pig-pig, su-su-su," to get them trotting to the feeder. I clean their pen and listen to their grunts. Glory and I walk along Furnace Road twice a day. Vehicles are rare, and we can hear them before they are upon us. We move into the weeds and let them pass. We have not walked beyond the fence in many weeks. The For Sale sign has disappeared, but I have not seen the small, red pickup truck.

A second towering white cross appears just inside the fence line. Pastor Dixon will not be a friend. However, there is probably no harm in a man who believes he was called to an untamed God's country.

§

Glory is facing the door, barking. This is not her quick, excited yip when the house is quiet, and she hears a noise that does not occur again. This is a bottomless warning from her chest. Her mouth gapes with the effort, opening and closing with teeth bared. She has never done this before. Her ears and tail are pressed back, and her body is taut with energy. I do not placate her with the singsong, "I hear it, good girl," that I use to thank her for protecting me. My stomach begins to tighten. This is the first time I've thought of removing the old rifle from the hall closet since Carter left. I lean it against the wall next to the front door. I move into the kitchen to look out the window. Pastor Dixon's truck is parked at the fence, but I do not see anyone in our yard. I want to step onto the porch with Glory. I want her next to me, but I do not think I can keep her by my side.

I open the front door and look through the screen door. It feels safer to be inside than out until I can identify what Glory has alerted me to. She presses her nose to the screen, sniffing rapidly. I cannot see the reason for her alarm. I would like to cradle the rifle in my arms, leash her, and let her lead me toward her distress. Our two acres seem vast. The barn and the backyard, both usually as safe as a nest, feel foreign and unprotected with Carter so far away.

"I looked, and behold, a black dog." I turn toward the voice. Glory barks, deep and throaty. "And his name was Death, and Hades followed with him." Pastor Dixon comes from the back of the house and stands at the bottom of the porch steps.

"What are you doing here?" I use Carter's voice of authority that Glory listens to. "What do you want?"

"When I was on the road from Tennessee, I dreamed a black dog would curse my land. It's rightfully mine but the sale fell through. A black dog's a bad omen, and you've been all over my land with that dog of yours." I close my fingers into fists. My fear turns to anger. A stranger with a dangerous fixation on my closest companion is trespassing on my land.

"We have nothing to do with that. That land's been

for sale as long as I can remember."

"I was led here, and I mean to get that land at any cost. Those crosses prove a man of God has staked his claim, and I know you've seen them on my land."

"Glory didn't do this to you," I respond with incredulous disbelief. His brow is set into hard, angry lines, and his eyes are wide and shiny. It is difficult to imagine an adult believing a dog could impact anything more than a game of fetch. He is no longer someone I want to maintain a congenial relationship with, and he has worn out his welcome. "You get off my land. You're trespassing on private property."

He ignores my command and takes a step toward the porch. Glory begins barking again. Her nose presses against the screen. He looks at her through the screen door. "Power was given to man to kill with a sword and with death, that beast of the earth." I can tell he has used this voice to preach fire and brimstone. Glory has begun to growl, a guttural, rolling sound, something darkly submerged that has been startled awake. I do not recognize this as the dog who sleeps at my feet and eats from my grandmother's wedding china. He climbs the steps and in one stride, crosses the wooden boards. We are face to face.

Glory lunges through the screen. She leaps at him, and they tumble down the porch steps. Neither of us expected the screen door would fail to keep Glory's fury inside the house. He falls onto his back in the grass. She is on top of him. My fingers close around the barrel of the rifle before it registers that I have grasped it. I stand on the top step, screaming Glory's name, maybe leave it, or drop it. I try to summon Carter's voice for this, but he never gave those commands while holding a weapon. I realize my hands are correctly positioned on the rifle. I think of raising the barrel and shooting into the air. The noise would startle all three of us. Pastor Dixon stumbles to his feet, red-faced and yelling. His sleeve is torn. Glory's jaws lock around his calf. She is growling and her head thrashes from side to side. I have never seen this side of her. He kicks at her with his free leg, but the kicks do not find a purchase. His arms beat at her, but she is like a machine.

I have been standing dumbly with a weapon in my hand that I do not intend to use. Carter's useless voice rushes from my lungs. My throat is hoarse and raw from screaming Glory's name. Pastor Dixon and Glory move with accelerating, desperate urgency. There is an unexpected flash of silver in Pastor Dixon's hand. The weapon seemed to come from nowhere.

§

My ears ring. I am still holding the rifle. I think of the silver glint, but there is a blank spot in my memory after it. Pastor Dixon lies in the grass, legs bent at an awkward angle. A ragged red stain spreads over his tan, suede vest. It is impossible to think I have caused this. Glory stands over him, sniffing. He does not move to stop her. My throat is sore when I call out, "Glory, come." I collapse on the steps and set the rifle next to me. My hands are shaking. Glory now sits on the other side of me. My head is level with her head in this position. I wrap my arms around her body, pressing my face against her side. My throat tightens, and I weep with great, wracking sobs against her warm, black fur.

§

Glory licks my wet cheek from our perch at the top of

the steps. I look toward the dead man in my front yard and wipe at slobber and tears with the back of my hand. Carter's four-year sentence is nothing compared to what I would get for shooting a man at close range. A wave of vertigo overcomes me, and I place both of my hands on the floor to steady myself until it passes.

I tell Glory to stay, and I walk over to Pastor Dixon. The red stain covers most of his chest. I look away from him to Glory on the porch. She whines at me. I do not know anyone who could keep her if I went away. Carter would not have a home to come back to. He would see me next through my own smudged glass window. I look at Glory again, and I cannot leave her. I cannot lose the place I know Carter has kept in his mind as a comfort.

My heart pounds in my chest. I think of Ginny and Maggie in the barn. There is only one way I can stay sleeping in my own bed with Glory at my feet.

§

Pastor Dixon lies nude in a dirt patch in the backyard. His clothing is at the bottom of the metal barrel I use for burning trash and leaves. He looks no different than any other man in town. His calling to the land across Furnace Road is not evident. He does not look like a man who would come after a family pet and justify it by misquoting the bible to his advantage. However, he is both of these things. My pause to look at him does not signify a hesitation. It is only a way to help frame this thing I have done.

There is satisfaction in the rhythm of the upward heft, the swing, and the impact. The ax moves with muscle memory, but I am afraid to stop because I do not know that I can begin again.

The legs of my jeans are soaked. My boots are covered. My sweater is ruined. I strip off my clothing, wipe my face on an inside-out part of my undershirt, and dump everything into the burn barrel. I will drop in my undergarments and set the barrel aflame when I get back from the barn.

"Here, pig-pig, su-su-su," I call out to the girls. I am grateful they are undomesticated and did not learn their names or become my friends. At first, I was surprised at their appetites. Now, I am beholden to them for it. I do not watch them dine; there is a limit to what I can endure.

The sodden dirt patch in the backyard will need to be churned with the rake, maybe set on fire before I let Glory back there. The girls will not need dinner tonight.

§

Glory sniffs the red truck at the fence. "Leave it," I say, tugging her leash without slowing. She trots next to me, sniffing the weeds along the dirt track. The sun is climbing into the sky, but the morning air is cool. I would like to ease into our old rhythms of talking aloud to her about Carter, but I am silent. There is much to sniff after so long, and she would not be interested in my voice. When the truck is far from view, I slow our pace. Furnace Road is no longer visible, and we are no longer visible to it. We are close to the white cross at the end of the track. I brush my fingers along its rough surface as we pass. Nature will do the same. Its fingers have staked their claim to everything else on this land. The starkness of a white thing will be the first to go.

I am looking for a dead tree with jagged, bare branches, far beyond the wildlands Pastor Dixon was drawn to. The sun is high in the sky when we come to a wire fence line. The trees nearby are peppered with yellow signs that read, "Posted No Trespassing by Order of the Virginia Department of Game and Inland Fisheries." I scan for the tree, and Glory is content to sniff the ground. It is almost new to her. We have only come here once before.

The tree comes into view. I lead us toward a low rise in the earth nearby. She matches my pace, slower as we walk parallel to it. I am looking for a den dug into the hillock, long-abandoned the last time I was here. The entrance is thickly carpeted with dried, brittle leaves. An active den's opening would be clear, leaves crushed to make way for furry legs and warm bodies. I am relieved. Although this land is untamed and desolate, I do not want to seek out a second burrow. "Glory, sit," I say to her. "Stay." She will not move. There is nothing here to excite her.

I bend to clear the leaves from the entrance and let Carter's duffle fall from my shoulder into the weeds. I drop to my knees and peer into the den. The floor slopes downwards into darkness. I unzip the duffel and empty its contents into the entrance. I kick at Pastor Dixon's bones, filling the den's mouth. I sit and straighten my legs into the hole, the soles of my boots pressing them deeper inside. There is no resistance as they slide downward on the sloping floor. I hear a faint clatter, bone on bone, as they fall into a pile on top of the older bones already at the bottom. I scoop the leaves back into place and loop the empty duffel over my shoulder. There is nothing to distinguish this spot on state land from any other rise in the earth.

Glory and I follow the wire fence until the For Sale

land is in sight. The terrain begins to look familiar. We pass the cross. What can I tell Carter on a prison phone next month? I can say I watched over our two acres, and Glory and the girls, and the land across Furnace Road is still for sale. I cannot say Pastor Dixon dreamed of Glory, or that he was drawn to land he will never leave. Glory matches my pace as the red truck comes into view. I wonder if anyone will come for it before Carter gets home to see it for himself.

Bunny Man Bridge

I watched two small boys lean against my bumper. The younger one ran a toy car along the hood, and the older one scratched his crotch without looking to see who was watching.

"Those are Macy's kids," Mell murmured. "No manners, either one of them." I knew she was comparing them to her son, Alby, who was sitting on the curb next to them.

"They're just boys," I responded, remembering myself as a boy at their age and trying to sound casual. In any other parking lot, my car would blend in. However, at The Windwood Motel, it was the newest and most expensive. I'd become accustomed to standing out as I pulled into a parking space every day. Most of the other cars were a decade or so older, with scrapes, dents, and peeling paint that felt at home at a weekly motel. Some, like the Saturn with one shattered headlight, and the Lincoln Towncar with its peeling vinyl roof, were no longer being manufactured. In this parking lot, it made sense that little boys would want to be near my car.

Alby leaped up from the curb and ran over to us, as though he knew we were talking about them. "Can I have two quarters?" He held his open palm toward his mother, and my stomach seized. My head snapped to Alby's hand, and I inhaled sharply through my nose. I probably had a quarter in my pocket. I couldn't remember ever giving one to a kid, but that wasn't the thing. It was a kid asking for one, holding out his hand, and hoping for a quarter that got me.

Mell looked at me. She asked, "What's with you?" and

began digging in her change purse. She handed Alby two quarters, and we watched him run over to the Coke machine by the office. He did not look back at Macy's boys. "I need those for laundry this weekend," she said. "You okay?"

"All this stuff with Lucy brought up some memories," I responded. I waved a hand toward the courtyard and parking lot. "Being here doesn't exactly ward off the boogeymen, either." The asphalt was permanently cracked. Weeds created a puzzle-piece effect between the faded parking space lines. We were sitting on the steps to the second-floor balcony where both of our rooms were. There was a lacework of rust on my step, and the railing had rusted out at the base.

"By the time I got here, I didn't have no more boogeyman to bring up." The corners of her mouth turned upward in a smirk, but it was more pitying than unkind. She continued, "I'd told everything to about a million counselors and social workers. I try not to think about what Alby'll say when he's your age." I nodded. I knew what Alby would say when he was my age. I hoped by then, he'd have enough other memories to not want to reminisce about living in a motel when he was ten.

As far as I could tell, I was the only one renting a weekly room at The Windwood Motel by choice. The other residents, including Mell and Alby, were waiting for county housing vouchers, or something better to come along before their benefits ended. There were plenty of other single women and children. Aside from me, though, the only other men were either elderly or elderly and disabled. My childhood probably aligned with most of the other residents, but somehow, my path diverged from theirs. I felt out of place here, but inexplicably comfortable with Mell.

"What's up with you and quarters anyway?" she asked. "Dinner van's almost here. You eating tonight?" I looked up at her, sitting one step above me with the sun caught in her hair. The ends were a riot of crispy bleached yellow, and the dark roots were the color of root beer in a glass. The nightly County Services dinner van was often the only hot meal Mell ate during the day.

"I need to get there while it's still light, and I don't think you want to hear about me and quarters. You've got enough on your plate with Alby without hearing another little boy's story," I said.

"Try me. Keep talking until the van gets here. It's spaghetti night." She lit a cigarette. I could see the early fine lines around her mouth that would deepen with age, cigarettes, and weekly motels.

I glanced at my watch and decided on the short version. It was more about Lucy than me. It was also easier to talk about my little sister than get into my own stuff. "When I was ten and Lucy was six, my mom shacked us up with a guy named Queue—" I began.

"Real piece of work," Mell interrupted. "You mentioned him. I figure he's the ground-zero reason for everything Lucy did. It's gotta start somewhere, and six is just as good an age as any. Lucky he wasn't your dad."

I nodded. I never thought of luck when I thought of growing up, but Mell was right. It could have been so much worse. "When Queue got laid off, he spent my mom's savings on a vending machine route. It was one of those 'be your own boss, work your own hours' jobs where the only people making money are the ones selling vending machines to guys like Queue."

Mell and I looked toward the Coke machine at the

same time. Alby was sitting in the worn patio chair next to the machine cradling a soda in both hands. He looked like I did at his age: brown hair that needed a haircut a month ago, a sprinkling of freckles across the bridge of his nose, ears a little too large for his head, and forgettable brown eyes. I glanced back at Mell and began again. "He'd come home with these canvas sacks of quarters and sit in the living room rolling them. I don't remember how it started, but he had this thing with throwing quarters at us. He told us we could keep every quarter we caught."

"Like an allowance?" Mell asked and took a drag of her cigarette. She tilted her head upward, pursed her lips, and exhaled. A plume of smoke drifted over our heads toward the second-floor balcony.

"Nah, more like an excuse to cause bruises. I think it was one of Lucy's demarcation lines."

She rested her elbows on her knees and leaned toward me. "What does that mean?"

"A demarcation line is a boundary," I responded. "Before the vending machine route, there was a pretty bad night when Queue smacked our mom so hard she hit the floor. Later on, Lucy asked me why we couldn't move out. I told her our mom didn't have enough money to rent an apartment. She asked me if the two of us could leave, and I told her kids can't get that much money. When Queue said she could keep every quarter she caught, it was like a lightbulb went off. She was six, and quarters are a big deal at that age."

"Demarcation, I totally get it," she nodded in understanding. "A boundary between before and after. I see where this is going."

"That first night, both of us lined up. I was thinking about quarters for video games and action figures. What kid wouldn't want all the free quarters they could catch? Turns out, he had this move with his fingers, something like snapping that sent quarters flying like a slingshot. There was no way to catch them, and he had great aim."

Mell nodded again. She was probably picturing Alby standing before one of her exes with his hands out, hoping for a quarter not meant to be caught.

"I was a pretty skinny kid. The first one hit me in the chest, and it brought tears to my eyes. I didn't even see it coming. You can figure out the rest of that shitty game. I never got why Lucy'd let him talk her into that so often when my mom was at work. Thing is, Lucy never cried. It didn't occur to me until later that she probably thought she could get money for rent. She never asked me how much rent was, and I never stuck around to see how many quarters he let her pick up. I pretty much stayed in my room reading. I think I thought if he were busy with Lucy, he'd leave me alone." I glanced at my watch. It didn't feel good to talk about this. If I kept talking, it would be too easy to start in on how I never told Lucy to stop letting Queue do that or stood up to him. I didn't know Mell well enough to have that conversation with her.

"What did I tell you? Of course, that asshole was ground zero. I mean, a demarcation line. That's a good word. Some of the other things you told me about Lucy, this makes sense. She figured out money comes from shitty men with strings attached." She laughed, clipped, and without humor. "Haven't we all?"

I glanced at my watch again. I wanted to be anywhere but The Windwood Motel's third step from the bottom, reminiscing about my dead sister and how I hid in my room instead of saying anything. "I've gotta head out while there's still good light. I'll catch up to you later on." I stood and brushed a fine dusting of grit from the seat of my jeans.

"No problem, Spencer. I hope you find what you're looking for on that road."

"Thanks. Enjoy spaghetti night." I nodded, raised my hand in a half-hearted wave, and headed toward my car.

§

Every time I drove to Colchester Road, I thought about why I booked a room at The Windwood Motel. It was a relic in an unwalkable Virginia suburb, surrounded by chain restaurants, car dealerships, and strip malls. The motel was a masochistic version of coming full circle. Maybe I was reconnecting childhood dots as though I could put things right for Lucy and change who she was, or who she grew into. The Windwood was a tangible starting point. If I could go back, I could imagine whispering my room number into her ear as a cure-all before she stepped in front of an Amtrak on the Colchester Overpass three weeks ago.

When I was twelve, a social worker from Women's Services booked us a double room with a cot there. The neighbors had called the police one too many times, taking pity on my mother, who was porcelain doll pretty and younger than I am now. I was too young to understand what it would mean when my mother turned down the offer. The only thing I remember was her saying the motel maids would steal her things. She made up with Queue. I stayed in my room reading garage sale western novels, and Lucy tried and failed to catch quarters. Had we moved, Queue would have been long gone. Lucy would have grown into a different girl. The Bunny Man would have been placed in a box of memories about a dark time in our lives. We'd probably have thrown the box into a ditch on the way to a better place. Right now, I'd be at my shop in Newport, selling nautical antiques to tourists instead of driving to Bunny Man Bridge.

§

I got lost in my thoughts as I made a left onto Colchester Road. I pictured myself slowing the car and approaching the tunnel. A steep, ivy-covered hill rose on either side of it. The tunnel's narrow, domed entrance was built into stark, white concrete, bordered by thick, angled brick supports on either side. Train tracks ran over the tunnel; however, the hill was so steep that they were not visible from the road. Two cars could not pass each other inside the tunnel, and I doubted anything taller than the smallest U-Haul truck could get through.

I thought of driving through the tunnel, then making a U-turn in the closest driveway beyond it and driving back toward The Windwood. I'd driven this route and made the U-turn so many times I could picture the twin lintel stones in the center of the tunnel's arched brick opening on either side. I could never bring myself to pull off the road near the tunnel and get out of my car. I couldn't fathom standing in the road, looking up the steep hill toward the tracks, or even climbing the hill as Lucy did.

I had a brief, rational moment in which I imagined myself turning the car around before I got to the tunnel. The dinner van would be gone by the time I got back. Mell would be sitting on the steps smoking cigarettes while Alby played in the parking lot. Maybe they'd both be sitting on their beds watching television. I wanted to be near her instead of alone on a one-lane road staring up at a silent overpass. However, I couldn't think of much to say if I stopped by her room. I didn't want to tell her I kept driving to Bunny Man Bridge, but I couldn't get out of the car. I gripped the wheel and felt ashamed all over again. My inaction here was no different than reading westerns in my room while a childish rent money fantasy blossomed in quarter-sized bruises on Lucy's small body.

I drove around the familiar bend in the road, and the tunnel came into view. It was late spring, but I had a vision of the scene covered in snow, with bare, skeleton trees lining each side of the road. What if I was still making this useless drive six months from now, chasing daylight in the winter gloom? When would it end? The impulse to stop the car seized me like opening my eyes to a bright shock of sunlight. This close to the tunnel, the road was hardly wide enough for two passing vehicles. I pulled onto a narrow, grassy area bordered by a wooden fence, formerly white but gone to grey and chipped in the elements. I cut the engine and sat with my hands on the wheel for a moment. My windows were rolled down to catch the breeze, and the first thing I noticed was the silence. The road felt different, driving through the tunnel. I was always moving, attention half on the road, trying to take in the overpass, figure out Lucy, and watch for oncoming traffic at the same time. The low purr of the engine had always existed in the background. With the engine off, the experience was completely altered.

I stepped out of the car and stood in the road, facing the tunnel. I'd be able to hear a car long before it rounded the bend. An acorn or a small branch dropped from the treetops with a clattering sound. A distant animal picked its way through the underbrush. A breeze rustled the branches in the canopy. Lucy was momentarily forgotten until I heard a far-off rumble. It transformed into a deep roar, and it was upon me before I could process it. An Amtrak's silver nose became visible through the trees. Car after car rushed along the top of the overpass in front of me. The noise was deafening, a ravenous, anonymous creature. I could not move as something else shot through me, more powerful than the impulse to stop my car. Lucy might have stood in this spot and watched the same blurred red, white, and blue stripes on the silver cars. I could not imagine what she had been thinking as she stood there with the thunderous Amtrak pounding in her chest. It was inconceivable to put myself in her position.

The caboose appeared without warning and disappeared into the trees before I had time to register that the train had passed. The engine's roaring, mechanical fury subsided, then faded until the forest returned to silence. This was as close as I was ever going to get to Lucy in life or in death. I wanted to mark the occasion, but I came up short. I did not know what to do with my hands or my feet, and I stood motionless, breathing and listening for sounds or actions that did not come.

I turned away from the tunnel, got into my car, and turned the key in the ignition. It was easier than I thought it would be to start the engine and pull away from the scene. I gripped the leather of the steering wheel cover, thinking that I did not belong here. I'd built a life far from this road, far from the things Lucy kept from our childhoods. I pressed the gas pedal and drove too fast for the narrow, winding road, but I could not outrun the train I'd seen on the overpass.

I cursed myself again on the drive back, because pills and a good Irish whiskey seemed a more appealing way to go. Of course, I'd pick a quiet, easy end while tucked safely into my own bed. Who knows how far Lucy had driven to get here. I didn't even know where she was living in the month before it happened. This train was her old quarters, her back-talking and sneaking out, her running away, and dropping out of high school. This train was her years of subsisting on minimum wage or earning money worth far less than the price she paid for it. There was safety in drinking whiskey out of a vintage rocks glass from my shop and downing a bottle of pills. This was my childhood bookshelves, letting Lucy take the brunt because it was easier, and the way I'd abandoned the trappings of my upbringing. Pills were a stable, safe antique shop I co-owned on touristy Thames Street in Newport.

For me, The Windwood Motel was going back to the beginning, coming home to every shameful thing from my youth that I'd left behind and refused to identify with anymore. It was thinking I could fix things and make myself feel better about letting them get so bad in the first place. For Lucy, Bunny Man Bridge was an end to whatever she had been running from or running to, since the night we learned about it.

§

My mother's idea of quality family time was driving the backroads near home in Queue's work van. Lucy sat on my mother's lap. I sat on the floor in the back, fighting for space between loose tools, cases of soda and boxes of snacks for the vending business, and a carpet of dirt and pebbles. My mother played her favorite folksy rock music so often that we knew the words to every song. After dinner, Queue would balance a six-pack of Budweiser in the console, and we'd drive the two-lane roads ubiquitous to the far-reaching outskirts of the suburbs. On one of these trips, we learned about The Bunny Man.

The story was so cliché that if you've ever heard of an urban legend about a killer with a hook for a hand, you can tell The Bunny Man story as well as I can. Instead of a hook, he wore a bunny suit and used a hatchet. Queue began the story in the voice you use to exaggerate campfire tales, and he slowed the van to a crawl as we neared a tunnel we'd never driven to. He looked over at Lucy on my mother's lap and told her this was where The Bunny Man could be seen every night. I was old enough to be entertained by a good scary story, but Lucy was gripped. She began to whimper on our mother's lap, and her tears seemed to fuel him. My mother didn't ask him to stop.

He blurted out something like, "Did you just see him?" Lucy began wailing, and he laughed. For a few moments, we coasted along the road to her sobs. He rolled down his window, tossed out an empty can, and opened another beer. The van crept toward a darkened tunnel that was illuminated in the headlights, and Queue turned to my mother. I heard him mutter, "Watch this," and the headlights went dark. The van kept moving, and Lucy began to howl. Queue's laughter blended with Lucy's cries. My mother yelled something I could not decipher. I sat on the floor listening to Lucy and my mother, imagining myself as a cowboy in a darkened stagecoach, protecting my family from Indians. The greenish glow of the dashboard lights illuminated my mother's hand grasping Queue's shoulder. I could see Lucy's outline, hunched over and gripping my mother. In an explosion of sound, Queue bellowed, "It's The Bunny Man," and began to roar with laughter. The high beams came on a second later, and the van accelerated so forcefully that I fell backward. My glasses flew from my face and skidded to the back of the van. I found them on my hands and knees amongst the dirt that had pooled near the rear doors.

My mother never altered her ideas about quality family time, and we spent many hours in the van with a six-pack. We heard The Bunny Man story for years on these drives, whether we were on Colchester Road or further from home. Lucy stopped crying after a while. On particularly dark stretches of road, Queue might say The Bunny Man was waiting for her after school, behind the bathroom door, or under her bed. The story got old for me. Queue never tired of telling it, and Lucy never became immune. I did not have the courage to butt heads with Queue, but I did wonder about my mother. I could not figure out why she sat dumb and still with Lucy on her lap every time, mesmerized by a man in a bunny suit who was coming for her daughter.

§

It was dark when I pulled into a parking space in the courtyard. Mell's light was still on, but I didn't knock. I wanted company, but I didn't want to talk. We didn't know each other well enough to sit in silence. What could I even say, something about how I saw the train and I'd rather go out with pills?

The air in my room was stale. I should have been accustomed to the perpetual odor of cigarettes, despite the sizable non-smoking sign on the door. The carpet was stained in only a few places, the bed was reasonably comfortable on the left side, and the room was cheap. The blinds blocked both sunlight and the light from the neon sign on the edge of the parking lot. For all of these things,

I was grateful. I was getting used to the smell.

I took off my shoes and lay on the bed, thinking about the rounded nose of the Amtrak breaking through the trees. The sound shook the forest in that area, and I imagined it would be deafening from the tracks. I knew little about stopping a train in motion. It seemed like the type of math problem that plagued me in school. If a westbound train going seventy miles per hour meets a little sister on an overpass…

It was not worth pondering why Lucy did it. There were too many easy answers to choose from. We were never close, and I take full responsibility for that. Who'd want a big brother who violated the tenets of siblinghood, fleeing the moment his mother brought an alpha male into the picture? I can hardly say what Lucy went through back then because when things started up between her and Queue, I retreated to my room. I missed the endings of many television shows in those days. Aside from being drawn to the incredible violence getting hit by a train entails, I could not figure out why she chose that location. However, it was easy to compare the absurdity of my Windwood Motel homecoming with her Bunny Man Bridge suicide; both locations were a battleground boundary in our childhood. At least mine made sense. What could have been going on with her to drive her toward her own sad version of a homecoming?

A laugh track on Mell's television drifted through the wall. Alby cackled, and Mell said something over the noise of the television. She had her own demons, arguably worse than Lucy's, yet she was next door. Mell left her ex with nothing more than Alby and her purse and found her way to The Windwood. She could have been Lucy in another life. Surely she knew women like my sister. She would know what motivated women to grab their purses and flee, or stay and dig themselves deeper into holes that came to no good end.

§

The following morning, I stepped into the motel's office. Everything inside me that made sense told me this was a bad idea, but something small and powerful had grown teeth since I saw the train the day before. Things that used to seem right and logical, like not asking the motel clerk to check for Lucy's name in the registry, had become insignificant. I had to know if Lucy had also found her way back to The Windwood, drawn her own lines into a final full circle as I had.

The air in the office was damp and artificially chilly. The area in front of the counter was bare, and the gray linoleum floor was missing one tile. A bulletin board on the wall opposite the door held a bad photocopy in English and Spanish advertising prenatal care for expectant mothers. A color poster next to it showed a smiling worker with olive skin wearing an ambiguous polyester uniform. "Apply Today, Work Tomorrow" was arced above a short, bullet-pointed list and a 1-800 number in bold typeface. The front desk clerk sat behind a thick glass window with a sliding panel.

She was all bad skin, heavy eye makeup, and yesterday's ponytail, bundled into a tattered rust-colored sweater. I expected the yammering jaw of a gum-chewer or the raspy voice of a heavy smoker. Instead, her voice was clear and polite. "Can I help you?"

"I was wondering if you could check the registry for my sister. I think she might have stayed here three weeks ago. Lucy Burbage," I asked.

"County?" she asked.

"County?" I repeated with uncertainty.

"Was she with Fairfax County Human Services, or did she check in on her own? County records are confidential. Matter of fact, who'd you say you were, again?"

"Her brother." I fumbled for my money clip in the front pocket of my jeans, thumbing through a few bills to reach the cards in the center of the fold. I handed her my driver's license through the open window. "Spencer Burbage. I'm her brother." She examined my license, glanced at me, and handed it back.

"Can you please check the registry? She's not here now, and I don't need to know anything else. I only need to know whether she checked in three weeks ago." I hoped she would say the registry was private. Knowing Lucy slept in one of these beds that our mother was too good for would not help me put two and two together. I wasn't even sure what I wanted two and two to equal. I thought of Mell. She must have gone somewhere on her first night out of the house with only Alby and her purse. Did front desk clerks in motels like this have a duty to protect single women?

The clerk tapped a long, chipped purple fingernail on the counter. "I should be able to tell you whether she was here if she checked in under her own name." She looked from my face to my button-down shirt, tucked into my jeans, and back to my face. I'd recently gotten a haircut, and my beard was trimmed to what I imagined was a rugged look. "Customers like you and probably your sister, not everyone here would bother to check ID." She turned toward a large, ancient monitor and began tapping her nails on the keyboard. "We don't usually give this information out."

My stomach dropped a notch. I had not eaten breakfast, and it felt profoundly empty. I did not want her to find Lucy's name in the registry. However, if she said Lucy didn't check in, I'd assume she hadn't shown her ID. There was no right answer. I looked at my watch. The shop on Thames Street was open. I'd only been in Virginia for a week, but I needed to call the shop.

"How do you spell Lucy? Is it an I E?" Her fingernails hovered over the keyboard.

"With a Y. L… U… C… Y." I spelled. The clerk tapped. I waited.

"I'm sorry, but nobody named Lucy checked in. I looked up your last name just in case, but nothing came up. Could be she paid cash, but either way, she's not in the system," she responded. Her tone suggested this was not the first time a missing person had not been listed in the registry.

I thanked her and left the office, filling my lungs with fresh air. I could not name how I felt. It was empty and full to overflowing at the same time. There are no words to blend opposites like disappointment and relief and shower them over a person as though the feeling is the answer they were looking for. I wanted the clerk to find Lucy's name with the same meaningless desire that drove me into the office. Another part of me knew it was irrelevant. She was gone. It did not matter where she spent the night before she drove to Colchester Road. Picking up her trail like a hack detective was about me, not about her. Driving to the bridge every day was also about me, and I was ashamed of this.

I'd read all eighty-nine Louis L'Amour westerns and most of the dime store copycats by the time I was seventeen, while Lucy went toe to toe with Queue and our mother. I did nothing, yet decades later, I was in a motel trying to figure out… figure out what? I didn't even care why she did it. There was no note, but you could almost draw a straight line from the day she ran away from home to that train. The thing I didn't get was The Bunny Man Bridge.

I knew driving there was futile. Lucy did not leave a trail of breadcrumbs for me to find. There was nothing that would come into view if I looked at the overpass in the right light. This was not about my little sister. It was entirely about me. Every time I admitted that I hated myself.

§

I sat in a parking space across from the strip mall bagel place next door to the motel, brushing crumbs from my shirt. My fist constricted around the waxed paper wrapper as I thought of calling the shop. Getting more time off was not difficult, but quantifying the time I needed was. I imagined saying the words "another week" aloud. My chest tightened at the urgency of having only seven days to get right with Lucy's death. I gazed toward The Windwood and thought of Lucy sitting in her car, eating a bagel. Then I thought of Mell, who accepted a paper plate from the dinner van every night. I dialed the shop because I did not know what else to do.

"Hi Edward, it's Spencer." I was glad to hear a familiar voice that had nothing to do with Lucy.

"Hey there, you on the way back?" He sounded hopeful and glad to hear from me. "I've got to tell you about that crate we got from the Lawrence estate sale. The best thing in it's a ship's bell from 1889."

"I was actually calling to let you know I'll be another week. It's this thing with my sister." I braced myself. I'd just given myself a timeline I couldn't break. Edward was like a father to me, and I had things to do at the shop. I couldn't call a week from now and extend, regardless of how I felt.

"Take as long as you need. You know, I didn't even know you had a sister until you got the call. I'm sorry about everything."

"Thanks, Edward. I gotta head out now. I really appreciate this. I'll see you at the shop next week."

§

For two days in a row, I left The Windwood early and drove around. I drove past identical neighborhoods with scores of mid-century modern houses and similar brick entrance signage; The Knolls, Dorsett Woods, Cambridge Creek, Springbank Farms. I was counting the days in my remaining week in a now-or-never desperation. I had five days left to get this right and return to Newport with a clear conscience. Both days, I drove past Colchester Road without making the turn. Both days, I told myself things would come together with one more visit I wasn't ready for. I promised myself I would be ready soon. I replayed the sound of the Amtrak through the forest. The memory of its silver nose in the clearing as it rushed over the tunnel taunted me. It would look different to a person about to step in front of it, but I'd only seen it from the ground. True to form, Lucy faced danger while I watched from the sidelines.

Both days on the ride home, I imagined talking to Mell, but I did not have the words to say that twice I'd failed to make a left onto Colchester. There was no way to convey that I wanted an understanding to erupt inside me, but I could not bring myself to make it happen.

Heading back to The Windwood on the second day, with five days of inaction ahead, and two days of flaccid uselessness behind me, I had a flash of reason. How were five days enough to make sense out of hiding in my room and letting Lucy try to catch quarters alone? Maybe I needed five years of standing in the road, counting trains, and trying to decide which one my sister jumped in front of. Or perhaps I needed to go home now without stopping at the motel for my clothing. I had my phone and my money clip. Everything else was replaceable. Instead, I thought of Mell and pointed the car towards The Windwood.

She was between jobs and doing that thing people like to call "getting back on your feet." Alby didn't have a father or at least one in the picture. Everything they owned was either in her car or in their room. While Alby was in school, Mell went to the women's center for computer classes and mock job interviews. She'd mentioned getting a resume there as though it was a winning lottery ticket. The Windwood was a threshold, and her case manager was laying out stepping stones she could use to change her life. It was difficult to imagine her as the type of woman who would turn down a room at The Windwood, thinking more of the maids and her belongings than keeping Alby safe.

Mell was a bright, welcome diversion, but I always came back to Lucy's darkness. I don't know who Lucy had in her corner when she ran away from home. I had no idea what men or women she filled the years with, or who the Amtrak helped her leave behind. I had never been there for her. However, I was the only one who could have, and should have, been on her side. God knows what my mother was thinking by keeping us in that house. Maybe I was just as bad, holing up in my room and drowning out the yelling with my nose in a book.

§

"Are you heading out or staying for dinner? It's chili night," Mell asked, then took a drag on her cigarette. She pursed her lips and blew the smoke downwards toward the parking lot. Alby was in their room watching television with the door open. I could hear the sound of a gun battle and men calling others to action.

"I don't think I'm supposed to eat dinner from the dinner van. They probably have a headcount, and I shouldn't take away from someone else," I said. "I'm not in a hurry to leave, though. I stopped seeing the point when I gave myself an arbitrary deadline. What did I think was going to happen in a week?"

"What do you want to happen?" She turned up a corner of her mouth. I knew she did not expect an answer to her question. "Lucy's gone. What are you even doing out there?"

"I don't know if it's called closure or absolution. I keep going there, then not going there, and nothing's happened either way. The only thing I feel is guilty. I keep thinking something's going to happen, then everything I did and didn't do in that house will go away." I paused. Mell took a drag of her cigarette. Alby changed the channel, and a cartoon's opening theme music floated toward us.

"You think a little boy can stand up to a man? You think Alby could've done something to my ex when he was drinking? The only difference that would've made was that my ex would have hit Alby too."

This caught me off guard, and I paused before responding. "He would've grown up remembering he tried to help you. I left the room every single time."

"It was your mom's job to stop that asshole, not yours. You ever heard of a little kid who made a difference against two adults pulling in the opposite direction?" She ran a hand through her hair. She took a deep breath and exhaled like she was talking to a child. "This is my life. I lived that shit every day for too long, trying to make sure my little boy was okay. It's my job, not his. I'm the mother." She paused, and we looked at each other. "This thing doesn't make you less of a man." She leaned toward me and looked into my eyes. "You were not a man, Spencer. You were a child. Lucy is not your fault."

I opened my mouth to speak, but what came out was a soft squeak of a sigh. The truth in her words cut deeply, but they did not absolve me of guilt. However, the part of me that paid my taxes in February, drank enough water, and went to the gym three times a week knew she was right.

I felt a powerful urge to leave The Windwood and stood without looking at her. "I can't stay for dinner." I reached into my pocket for my keys and headed toward my car without bothering to brush the dirt from the seat of my jeans.

§

I made a left on Colchester Road. I did not think of the silence I experienced the time I stopped the car and got out at the overpass. I did not think of what the Amtrak's engine car looked like as it sped over the tunnel or the booming, mechanical resonance that filled the air until it passed. I concentrated on breathing. Mell's words stung with honesty as they replayed in my head, "You were a child. Lucy is not your fault." I could not think about where my car was heading or what I would do when I got there. Instead, all I could think of was what I'd just left.

In western novels, the cowboy hero prevailed in the end by protecting something he cared about at all costs. I'd grown up knowing there was a ranch to save or a family to protect from the Indians. Even stagecoach robberies were usually for noble causes; to make bail for an unjustly accused relative or pay off the land and make a home for your wife and child. Having a thing to take care of existed on the page, but I'd never thought to put it into practice. Opportunities may have arisen, but I'd been blind to them. I was single, without pets or even a house plant to water regularly. I could not think of one thing I'd protected or made an effort to impact.

The Colchester Overpass came into view. I slowed the car, then stopped it and killed the engine in the middle of the road. My heart began to pound in my chest. I pictured three scenarios: climbing the steep hill and standing on the tracks as the train broke through the trees; making a U-turn and getting on I-95 North toward Newport without stopping at The Windwood for my things; or figuring out the right thing to say, then standing in Mell's doorway and trying to make sure my words came out the way I meant them.

I paused and tried to breathe evenly. I was looking for a sign, but I knew nothing was coming. Queue's van was not going to appear in my rearview mirror. The Amtrak ran on a schedule that had nothing to do with me. Mell would smoke cigarettes, go to the women's center, and worry about what memories she was giving Alby. There was only one scenario I could affect. There were no entities but me that were capable of the forward motion necessary to finally do some good. I started the car, put it in reverse, and backed into the closest driveway. I did not want to drive through the tunnel, even for the very last time.

I thought of how to make my words mean what I wanted them to. I knew what I felt, but it was difficult to transfer the bursts of emotion and need into something that would resonate with Mell. She would get caught up in big words and paragraphs of exposition. A list of pros and cons seemed too much like a contrived negotiation. I considered pulling off the road to write my thoughts on a napkin from the glove box, but I was pulling into The Windwood's parking lot before I got that far. From my parking space, I could see her and Alby sitting on their beds watching television with the door open.

I climbed the stairs and stood in her doorway. She looked over and smiled from her perch on the bed. "How was it? You okay?"

"How was dinner? What did I miss?" I was glad for the distraction. The dinner van never ceased to be a topic of conversation.

"They had Frito's tonight with the chili. You ever heard of a thing called Frito Pie?"

I paused for a beat. I had one chance at this, but I did not have the right words for it. "Hey, Mell?"

"Yeah?" She tilted her head to the side and knit her brows. "What's wrong?"

"Have you ever been to Newport?" I asked. I did not know how else to begin.

"You're from there, right?"

"I have a three-bedroom cottage. It's small, but you and Alby can have your own rooms. You can see the water from the porch, and we can really use some help in the shop."

I could not read her expression. Her words were slow and calculated. "What are you saying, you want us to move in with you?"

"I don't know what I'm saying except that I won't hurt you or Alby." I wished I'd pulled over and taken notes on a napkin. "I'm not asking for anything but to give you a second chance. This could be a second chance for me, too. I thought I was going to get one driving to the bridge, but Lucy's gone, and you're not."

She looked at me without speaking. Her chest rose with a deep inhalation, and her chest and shoulders fell with the exhale. I wanted to speak to break the silence, but she spoke first. "What is this, Spencer? You haven't even made a move on me, and now you want to move in together?" Her voice took on a harsh tone. "You gonna ask me to move into your bedroom when we get up there?"

My heart sunk. She had the wrong idea about everything. "Remember mentioning the kind of memories Alby's going to have when he's my age? You don't even know where you're going when you leave here." She looked over at Alby, who was still immersed in the television. "I can change those memories for him and for you too. I can make a difference, Mell, which is what I should have done when I was Alby's age." I paused to catch my breath. My palms were sweating, and I wiped them on my jeans.

"I don't know if my car will make it that far, and how do we get back if it doesn't work out?"

"I'll give you an advance on your paycheck." I reached into my pocket for my money clip, but she smirked and rolled her eyes. I grinned at her, and her face softened.

"The only thing I want is a chance, Mell. You took Alby and came here because you wanted one too. My own mother didn't even do that. I don't think either of us knows what a second chance really looks like, but I'd like to find out."

She put a hand to her mouth, but I could see the wide smile behind her fingers. "Alby, do you like your school?"

He was absorbed in the television and had not looked over at me. He answered Mell without looking at her. "Not really. I know we're moving, so I didn't make any friends." She looked from him to me and back to him.

"You want to finish the year in a cottage?" She tucked a strand of hair behind her ear and smiled at me with her eyes as well as her mouth. Alby nodded without looking over. His answer in the affirmative was drowned by a sitcom laugh track. Mell looked from him to me, then paused while holding my gaze. "Okay," she said without ceremony. "We'll come."

My stomach fluttered but my voice was steady. "Let's leave tomorrow."

I looked at the little boy on the bed next to Mell. His memories were about to change from social services and weekly motels to a cottage on the Atlantic coast. I had been to Bunny Man Bridge and I had seen the Amtrak, but I understood neither. For the first time since arriving in Virginia, I knew that understanding those two things no longer mattered.

Dating Silky Maxwell

Summer.

Winston's final song echoes inside Ella's head. She can only remember the chorus, "I'm every woman, it's all in me…" She allows the words to play on a loop, savoring the wisps of his performance. The door clicks closed behind her and she pauses in the foyer, calling out, "Perkins." She separates the syllables, drawing out the *r* and the *innn*. She hears his feet on the hardwood floor, jumping off the bed and running to greet her before she sees him. "Good boy," she says, crouching to stroke the large, black cat who is purring and rubbing his body against her boots. She places her purse and keys on the floor and runs both hands along his back. "I'm every woman, you're a black cat," she sings, changing the lyrics to the song she cannot get out of her head. He looks up at her and she continues to pet him. He meows once and walks into the kitchen with his tail held high. "You had your dinner before I left and it's too early for breakfast," she calls to his back.

She stands, picks up her purse and keys, and sets them on the slim, polished dark wood table near the door. She walks through the living room, an expanse of dove gray walls with dark wood furniture and red accents, and into her bedroom. Twin framed Diane Arbus photos above the couch, a shirtless young man in suspenders with a crooked smile, and a woman in a house dress shielding her eyes from the sun, look down on her as she passes. Once in the bedroom, she sits on the black and gray abstract patterned comforter and begins removing her fire engine red patent leather boots. They're the same shade as the short, bobbed wig she removes and places on a Styrofoam wig head on her dresser. Her dress lands on the floor and she rakes her fingernails through her shoulder-length brown hair, shaking off the sensation of her scalp being constricted beneath a wig for many hours. Her arms slip into a fluffy robe, a gift from a fan. Perkins is meowing and she follows the sound into the kitchen. It is too early for breakfast, but it is not too early for the salmon treats he loves. She shakes three from the container and lets him eat them from her palm.

She begins to prepare a mug of chamomile tea and notices she is still humming Winston's song. She does not mind the earworm. She could be halfway to falling for him. It is too soon to know, but it is not too soon to savor accompanying him when he performs. She knows his secret is performing in drag. He knows her secret is Silky Maxwell. Everything else, she's beginning to believe after three dates, will fall into place. His dress, though, she thinks, wrinkling her nose at the mauve taffeta. "You're the best mother of the bride that DC drag has ever seen," she'd said to him while they were getting ready at his townhouse.

"And you're the best at not using this outfit to get more likes or followers. Are you even allowed to go out without posting it?" he responded, tugging at the hem of her short, black, vintage slip, worn as a dress. They'd both laughed and turned back to the mirror. He glanced at his watch and commented on the time. He didn't go on until after 10:00 p.m., and there was no reason to arrive at the bar before 9:00 p.m.

How does it look, she wonders, to see her and Winston together? At first glance, beneath the streetlights in the summer darkness, they could be a prim mother and a rebellious daughter. However, mothers rarely take their daughters to Dupont Circle at night, a neighborhood full of gay bars, nightclubs, late-night restaurants, and a thriving drag scene.

She brings her tea into the living room. Perkins jumps on the couch and she sits next to him. He nestles closer to her and she can feel the warmth of his body on her thigh. The tea is too hot to sip. She sets it on a coaster on the coffee table, a low expanse of polished, ebony wood that compliments the table in the foyer. Her mind wanders from Winston's dress to the first time he invited her to his townhouse to get ready to go out.

"This is Deirdre's closet if you can call it that." His fingers curled into air quotes at the word closet. He led her into a spare bedroom. Two steps in, she froze. Winston's drag persona, Deirdre, was not the stunning, theatrical Glamazon she imagined on their first date when he told her he performed in drag.

Shelves lined one wall of the room. One shelf was filled with wigs in shades of dirty blond, auburn, and middling, average brown. They were mostly curly and shoulder-length or shorter, reminiscent of a cafeteria lunch lady. Had Winston brought her to his grandmother's house? Her stomach began to tighten.

Another shelf was full of sensible shoes in muted shades of brown and navy, white sandals with Velcro straps, and one pair of black pumps with chunky heels. Sturdy, utilitarian leather handbags with thick straps filled the final shelf. "Do you impersonate Mrs. Doubtfire?" She was incredulous at the display, comparing it to an old Robin Williams movie in which a man poses as a dowdy housekeeper.

He laughed. "I'm sorry about the surprise. I know what people think when they hear the words drag queen."

Her hands were on her hips and her brow was furrowed in indignation. She flashed back to her initial excitement at meeting Winston, another person with an enormous secret he could not share. She'd imagined them as co-conspirators, but her hopeful expectation now felt like a huge weight. This wasn't the wardrobe of someone who would be a close companion. "Surprise is right. What's your deal, Winston?"

"Everyone does glamour, but nobody does real. Look at me. I have a five o'clock shadow at 4:30. I'm tall and lanky, and my hands and feet are huge." He held his hands toward her. His fingers were long, and his knuckles were prominent and hairy. She looked from his hands to his face. His jawline, which she'd found handsome on their first date, was just that; handsome, masculine, and pronounced. There was nothing soft or feminine about him. "I'm most comfortable as a version of myself in a dress. Deirdre's a bit of a parody." He motioned to the open closet door. Ella took in a row of dresses in muted colors. He stepped toward the closet and pulled out a floral printed dress with a ruffle at the neck. He held it against himself with pride. The dress fell to below his knees. "As a woman, this is who I'd be in twenty years." Ella didn't speak. She looked from the dress to the shelves, and back to him. They were silent for a moment as he hung the dress next to a black dress with sheer, lace sleeves. "Are you okay?"

"I'm sorry, I'm just surprised at your look. I thought we had something."

"We do. Do you know what would happen at work if anyone saw me? It doesn't matter whether I'm dressed like a Vegas showgirl or wearing a polyester pants suit. I'd be screwed either way. I know you understand."

She relaxed. Winston was right. He'd accepted her, and she must accept him in kind. Drag is drag, no matter how silly he must look on stage. "I'm going to be a little overdressed tonight. I was thinking of costumes when I packed." She brought a short, hot pink wig and three of Silky's outfits.

"You're going to upstage Starla Cranberry, and that rarely happens. I'm wearing black and white tonight. Do you have something that matches?"

She smiled. The pink wig would keep her from being recognized. It was thrilling to think of going out partially dressed as Silky, while still being known as Ella. She looked at Winston. Something softened inside her. He was the first person who accepted her as both Ella and Silky. "Absolutely," she said.

There are so many reasons to like him, she thinks, taking a sip of her tea. It is still hot but manageable. She works a few hours a week in a small, independent bookstore for the W2 and the sense of normalcy going to work affords her. Her hair is brown, a shade her grandfather called shit brindle. It's fine and limp and won't hold a curl. Her brows are pale and thin, and her eyes are a washed-out blue. Yet, she's a controversial influencer with almost a million social media followers, but few real friend. Fully made up, Silky Maxwell is everything Ella learned was wrong, growing up as the only child of two parents immersed in dinner parties, Miss Manners, and keeping up with the Joneses. The personality she's created would devastate them. Her father is the principal of the city's exclusive, private high school where government officials, diplomats, and local celebrities send their children. He'd be forced to explain her lifestyle to the board if she were discovered, and her mother would be humiliated in the scandal. She loathes to consider the consequences. Winston has a prominent job on The Hill in the buttoned-up world of Washington, and a penchant for lip-synching in drag bars. He's the first person she's met with as much at stake if their secrets were revealed.

She sighs with the wonder of it all, considering how a first date and a daring confession on his part, "What do you think of men in drag?" transformed into her sharing Silky Maxwell with a stranger. They closed down the bar that night. The words tumbled out between them, and she told him about the photoshoots and sponsors, the videos, and the fans.

She laid herself bare between sips of wine, even mentioning that Silky Maxwell was a combination of the name of her first pet and her mother's maiden name. "How did you get started?" he asked, leaning back in his chair, awaiting a salacious adventure. "Mine probably came from hiding in my mother's closet when I was in preschool."

"Years ago, a girlfriend asked me to do a photo shoot for a contest she wanted to enter."

He laughed. "And you were discovered? That's classic."

"Kind of. You know that old pinup queen from the fifties, Bettie Page?" He nodded, and she continued. "Turns out, I'm a dead ringer for her if I put on a corset and a black wig with bangs. Who knew? Anyway, my friend's photo won the contest, and that led to another photoshoot. They asked me to tag the makeup brand on social media, and I couldn't believe how much they paid me. I was working full time at the bookstore but I was pretty broke back then so it seemed like a ton of money. Today, I wouldn't get out of bed for that amount." She laughs, and Winston chuckles. She takes a sip of wine and continues. “Everyone’s heard of influencers, but I didn’t realize it was happening to me until I was making more money from social media than from my full-time job. Fast forward, and here I am.”

Perkins has fallen asleep beside her on her robe. His purring is a low, steady rumble. She strokes his fur, not wanting to get up and wake him.

§

“I know he’s not gay, but I’ve never run into such a gentleman before.” Ella sighs. She closes her eyes as Cassie, the makeup artist and her closest friend, begins brushing shimmery gray eyeshadow onto her lids.

“Girl, I know you’ve heard the phrase, ‘He’s just not that into you,’ and you know what I think?”

“Stop it, Cassie,” Ella chides without opening her eyes. “We’ve been out like seven times. I know he’s into me. You know how you can just tell that about someone?” Cassie utters something in the affirmative, but it’s laced with sarcasm. “I never thought I’d run into the frumpiest queen in DC. Maybe he’s also the nicest.”

“Nice is one thing, but how long do you think it’s normal to go before you have your first kiss? Okay, open.”

Ella opens her eyes. She blinks into the brightness of the lighted mirror and examines her makeup. “We always go out made up. Do you think either of us wants to smudge our lipstick by kissing?”

§

Ella pulls the pie from the oven. The lattice crust is uneven, so thin in spots that the blueberry filling covers some of the lattice sections entirely, leaving dark, uneven blobs instead of neat squares. This is her first attempt at lattice crust. She wishes she'd practiced weaving the strips over, under, over, under until they were aligned perfectly before putting the pie in the oven. Instead, she straightened them with her fingers. Three dough strips tore while she was weaving them, but she pressed them together and continued to weave until they covered the pie's surface.

She snaps a photo of the pie, then taps, adjusts, and scrolls through the photo editing filters until the pie's colors are warm and rich. She uploads it and adds her signature hashtags, then a few she's never used; #bakingislife, #realness, and #blueberrybabe. She takes a few bites of the pie, and then places it beneath a heavy glass dome on her kitchen island. She loves baking, but she has never revealed this to her fans as Silky. It is exciting to share a small part of herself as Ella, even if it is only one photo. Everything about Silky is contrived to feed her followers, but this pie is a real thing.

Her phone begins to chime as she's finishing the dishes. She scrolls through the comments. Her fans are usually kind, and she has learned to ignore mean-spirited comments that come with her influencer status. However, negative comments have always been about something fake. Today, they are about Ella.

"OMG what happened? Poor pie."

"Women belong in the kitchen, but you don't."

"Hope it tastes better than it looks."

She sets the phone down. It continues to chime. She presses and holds the button on the side until it is silent.

§

Ella grasps Winston's hand. It is after last call, and

people are streaming out of the bar. "Your last song was excellent. I mean, I know the song, but I've never thought about it that way."

Winston sings the chorus in an off-key baritone, "Man, I feel like a woman..." The air is warm and muggy. The bars along the street are emptying, and the sidewalks are filling.

"The crowd in there was crazy tonight." She takes his hand in hers and squeezes. He squeezes back, and then he pulls his hand from her grasp. They reach a corner and wait for the light to change. "Do you want to come back to my place?"

His lips form into a weak smile in response. His skin has a sallow cast in the streetlight's orange glow, and his lipstick is wearing off. She presses her lips together, imagining that her own has also worn off. They've always parted company after his performances, and Cassie's words ring inside her head.

"I'm going to head home," he responds.

"Alone?" She looks up at him through her thick, false lashes. She imagines facing the camera, an invitation to her fans, and now, to him.

"I think you're great, really great."

Her expression drops, and her shoulders sink. "But?"

"I'm sorry if I led you on. I love hanging out with you—"

"But what? We've been going out for almost two months."

"This isn't dating. This is just two performers going out in costume. I don't think I gave you any other signals." He clears his throat. "This influencer thing you do is distasteful," he says.

"Distasteful?" she spits in disbelief. Her hands fly to

her hips. She has not judged him for dressing like a spinster aunt. In fact, she's embraced it. "What's distasteful about me?"

"Taking most of your clothes off to get followers and then pushing brands you don't believe in." He plucks the long strand of pearls away from his padded chest and holds them in his fingertips for emphasis. "Deirdre's a part of me but you're just in this for the money. It's fine for us to dress up and stay out late at night, but I have a whole life away from this." He lets the strand fall to his chest. "You don't."

She looks at him in disbelief. His wavy, auburn wig is frizzy, and the part is off-center. "What are we?" It's one thing for him to hold an opinion of her job, but it's another thing to judge her as Ella for it.

"Nothing, Ella. Just friends."

She doesn't speak. The light has changed. People pass them on both sides, but neither of them moves. Her eyes fill with tears, and her body feels heavy. She knows not everyone embraces Silky Maxwell, but maintaining the separation has never been difficult. She sees the occasional negative comment about Silky on pop culture websites, but they haven't been directed toward Ella. She shared her real personality with him. He's blurred the line, calling her out for embodying a fictitious character whose principles he does not agree with.

If their outings weren't dates, he was never a kindred spirit. Instead, Deirdre and Silky might as well have been dating. The idea of meeting her counterpart on a first date now seems ridiculous. She looks down at the sidewalk. A tear falls from her eye onto the toe of her red patent leather platform boot.

He steps toward her with arms outstretched. She doesn't want him to hug her. Who is he, anyway? He is a man dressed in a costume, calling her out for her own costume. She wants to yell at him that Silky Maxwell and Deirdre are not even real. How can he judge her for something she made up when he's done the same thing? She steps away from him, shaking her head. "You're right, Winston. We're nothing." The light has changed to green in the opposite direction of her condo, but she crosses the street anyway. She wipes the tears from her cheek with the back of her hand. She doesn't look over her shoulder when she reaches the other side of the street. Winston doesn't want her, but there is a whole world on her screen who does.

§

Fall.

"My apple pie won a prize. I love silent movies. I know the words to most yacht rock songs. Touching animal rescue videos make me choke up."

She deletes the last sentence. She scrolls to the top of the page and considers her alias for the fifth time in an hour. Ella Just Ella. It is difficult not to include Silky in this profile and call herself something like DangerElla13. She scrolls to the bottom of the screen and stares at the Upload Photos button. She has thousands of photos to choose from and none at all. Her fingernails tap erratically on her desk. There is no way to complete her profile without uploading at least one photo.

It's against her instinct to hold the phone at arm's length and snap selfies without makeup, without at least looking in the mirror first. It's against her instinct to take a picture of herself in her bedroom's full-length mirror in yoga pants and the frayed college t-shirt she's had for years.

It's also against her instinct to upload the photos to the app and tap the Complete Profile button. She does these things anyway, one after the other until there's no going back from it. What you see is what you get, she thinks. Her hands begin to shake, but it isn't with nervousness. Instead, it's exhilaration. She's never been on a dating site. A week ago, it would have been unthinkable to post photos like this publicly. The prize-winning apple pie changed everything.

She'd entered her special occasion apple pie in the farmer's market's annual end-of-season bake-off last weekend. She dropped off the pie, filled out a contact card, and forgot about it. The pie was always a crowd-pleaser, but she assumed she was competing against professionals.

Three days ago, she received a cheery email informing her that she was the winner. A wave of joy bloomed in her chest. She read the email twice. She called Cassie, eager to share the news with a real person. Cassie didn't answer, so she left a message. It began with, "I know this sounds silly, but…"

Cassie responded a moment later. Her words held more weight than a text message had the right to carry. "Can't talk now. Don't post that! Silky Maxwell doesn't bake pies."

Ella sank to the couch. Silky Maxwell was a happy accident of good genes, not a real person. Her pie won, but she had no one to tell. However, if she put on a new bra, tagged the designer, and shared it with her fans, the photos would be liked, commented on, and reposted many times over. Sometimes it felt like she was little more than a vehicle for Silky Maxwell. This rarely bothered her, but now, she couldn't stop thinking about it. She'd won a prize, but she couldn't own the accolades.

§

The dating app chimes. A man's photo appears on her screen beside his message, "Tell me you prefer Buster Keaton to Charlie Chaplin, and we're a match." Keaton is one of her favorite silent film actors. She clicks the photo and scrolls through his profile. He's a big guy, maybe 6'5". His face is wide and fleshy. His neck is broad, and his shoulders fill the frame. He outweighs her by far more than one hundred pounds. In another picture, he stands behind a man who appears dwarfed by his girth.

It strikes her, not being able to share the news of her pie, that she's cultivated a thing of great shallowness she cannot escape from. Silky Maxwell doesn't bake pies. Instead, Silky is a painted thing of beauty, a fantasy form whose only purpose is to put on lingerie and makeup and endorse products. This man reached out to her and wasn't put off by her unflattering photos. She won't be shallow and allow herself to be put off by his photos, either. They share an affinity for silent films. Maybe there are more mutual interests to discover.

She types, "Keaton did all his own stunts, mostly in one take. He beats Chaplin every time." They trade messages until late into the evening. Silky Maxwell doesn't come up; Silky has nothing to do with one-hundred-year-old movies, or pies, or the fact that they both know the words to every song on Paul Simon's Graceland album. She should have guessed that from his alias, "Call Me Hal."

On the second night, Hal tells her "Three Ages" was the first silent movie he ever saw. She tells him she laughed in that *Rin Tin Tin* movie when the condor snatched the baby. He tells her he did, too. Neither can remember the movie's title. He admits to laughing during the dramatic parts of *Nosferatu*. She smiles, and types that she also laughed. They stay up late again. She learns he's a cameraman for one of the local morning shows when he says he has to be up for work in three hours.

"Ella Just Ella, so glad I reached out yesterday."

"I am, too. Send me your top three films tomorrow."

"Will do. Signing off. Have a great night."

She thinks of him the following day and wonders what films he will send.

On the third night, he sends the list. She responds with one of her own. They learn that they were both bullied in junior high. He tells her he had a sister who died before he was born. She tells him she always wanted a sibling but had an imaginary friend instead. She lies in bed, thinking of him that night.

On the fourth night, she admits she felt weird in high school because her parents were still married and loved each other. She learns his parents divorced when he was three. His mother remarried a kind man who was an excellent father. She taps, "I thought about you today."

"Good or bad?"

"Good. I'm still here." She pauses, cursing herself. She's thought about Hal every day. They share so many interests, and he's easy to talk to. This feels real, not last summer's manufactured facade of two performers going out in costume.

Hal's response appears. "Would you like to meet for dinner? I'll come out your way."

"OMG I'm so glad you finally asked." She feels like she's known him for years, and it's exciting to think of meeting him in person.

He responds, "I wanted to ask the day you said you

laughed at the condor snatching the baby. Do you have a favorite spot for dinner?"

She knows people at a few chic restaurants and lounges, but none of them are right for her first date with Hal. She wants him to see a part of her she would never share with her fans. "Are you okay with a hole in the wall?"

"I'm up for anything."

Her chest flutters again. She scrolls through his profile and studies his photos. She can see the sincerity in his eyes. His face is large and the skin beneath his chin is loose, but he isn't unattractive. He's also kind and funny. She can't wait to meet him.

§

Ella arrives at Los Guapos early. The restaurant is a dingy, forgettable storefront in a neighborhood where real estate is affordable, and gentrification is years away. It's her favorite restaurant to go to with Cassie after shoots, and the food is authentic. She leans against the brick facade and scrolls through Hal's profile as she's done dozens of times. She alternates nervousness with excitement and wonders what his first words to her will be. Silent movies don't have quotes fans can swap. She knows he's tall, and wonders if she will even come up to his shoulder. She's five foot one on a good day. Should she make a joke about her height? How cliché, she thinks. Should they shake hands when he arrives? Is that too formal for people with this kind of connection? She purses her lips, going over their conversations for an inside joke he'll recognize. Her stomach is in a knot with nerves. It's been years since she related to someone on this level independently of Silky Maxwell. She likes Hal, and she wants him to like her.

"Ella just Ella..."

She turns toward the deep voice behind her. Hal is standing close to her on the sidewalk, and she takes a step backward. He towers over her petite, slender frame. She knew he was a big guy, but she wasn't prepared for this. More perplexing is that he does not look like his photos, which must be more than a decade old. Her stomach drops. In her excitement to get to know someone without wearing makeup or being Silky Maxwell, they neglected to compare ages. She pegged him for late-thirties and didn't mind a ten-year age gap. She remembers checking the box for men as old as their forties on a whim, but even forty-nine would be a stretch for Hal. He holds a broad hand toward her, smiling. "I'm so glad to finally meet you, Ella. Hal Mulvaney, at your service."

She smiles at him and takes his hand, remembering her manners and their connection. "So nice to finally meet you, Hal." Her hand disappears into his warm grasp. She's silent for a moment as he pumps her hand up and down. She looks at the restaurant's dingy storefront as though seeing it for the first time. "I know how this place looks, but you can't get food like this anywhere else." She motions toward the restaurant. A couple exits. Mariachi music wafts through the open door. Hal releases her hand and steps to catch the door before it closes.

"After you," he says, looking into her eyes and smiling. She returns the smile and turns away to enter the restaurant. The scent of chili powder and grilled meat envelops them. The cozy, dark wood and tile interior have always made her feel welcome, but her face drops as she takes it in with Hal behind her. The available tables are small and intimate, and Hal is too large for a table that only seats two.

She turns back to him. "We don't have to eat here."

"Are you kidding? It smells delicious. Table for two, please." He looks over her head at the host who has approached them. She turns toward the host and smiles with her mouth closed, but the host is not looking at her. He takes two menus from a stack and looks over her head at Hal. "Follow me."

The host leads them through a doorway with "La Fiesta" painted over the door frame in scrolling, red letters. They're seated at a spacious table for four in a room full of empty tables. A red, white, and green piñata dangles from the ceiling in one corner, and three giant, ornate burgundy sombreros with gold beaded trim hang on the walls. Ella is embarrassed for suggesting this restaurant. "I'm sorry, I–"

"I know what you're thinking but look around. We've got a private room to ourselves. You don't get that every day." Hal's smile is genuine. However, it accentuates the lines on his face. Ella returns the smile. He is making the best of sitting in a back room, she thinks, and I'll do the same.

"So Chaplin versus Keaton, what are the odds you'd meet someone on an app who actually has an opinion?"

"I know," Hal responds with a laugh. "I used to go to this old theater in Maryland that had a silent film series and an original Wurlitzer. I haven't been since my schedule changed at work."

Ella grins, remembering the long evenings they spent chatting. She feels connected to him once again. "The Weinberg Center in Frederick. Last year was the first year I didn't get season tickets."

"What a small world. We should go."

The waitress appears at their table before Ella can answer. They both order margaritas. Hal glances at his menu. "What's good here?"

"I always get the tropical platter. I don't think I've ever ordered anything else." He nods and bows his head to the menu. She holds hers as though studying it but considers him instead.

His form fills most of his side of the table. His hair, a dark brown in his photos, is all salt and pepper. His forehead is etched with lines, and there are two deep creases between his untamed brows. Marionette lines run from his nose to the corners of his mouth, then extend toward his chin. His gray stubble implies that he did not shave, rather than indicating that he is cultivating a beard. She cannot imagine cradling his doughy, middle-aged face in her palms and pressing her lips to his. She clenches her jaw. Meeting Hal, an earnest and affable person she thought she'd love to get to know, was not supposed to go like this. She thinks of the unflattering photos she used in her profile. The word shallow resonates inside her head, but it is not directed toward the fans who wouldn't accept her real self or her blueberry pie. Her temples begin to ache from clenching her teeth. The word *shallow* is directed toward herself.

§

"Can you please let me out here?" She is in the back of an SUV rideshare, stopped at a light twelve blocks from home.

The driver turns around to look at her. "I can't do a refund. It's gonna charge your card the whole amount."

"That's fine. I just need to get out." A walk home in the crisp fall air will help her sort out her feelings about dinner with Hal. She exits the SUV and steps between two parked cars to the sidewalk. She's in a residential area, away from the noise of evening traffic.

She repeated the word shallow to herself like a mantra when her mouth was full at dinner. She'd felt a connection with Hal and the difference in their sizes was easy to overlook. It seemed almost irrelevant in light of the way he made her feel. Seeing him in person was a shock, not at all how he presented himself on the app. Yet, she'd clung to their connection through dinner, beating the word shallow into her brain. Her fans are shallow. They'd never have built her into who she is today if she'd tried to do it as Ella. She doesn't want to be that way with Hal. She knows how much it hurts to think she wouldn't be accepted unless she was in costume. It's unthinkable that she'd be that narrow-minded with someone else, especially a kind, sincere man like Hal.

Sincere. She feels the word in her stomach like a blow. What would be sincere about putting Silky's photos on the app, and showing up nearly unrecognizable as Ella in jeans and limp, shit-brindle hair? Yet, Hal has done this to her with dated photos that he hardly resembles.

Everyone's taught it's the inside that counts. It is easy to connect appearance to attraction, but she blurred the line for Hal. Does her reaction to his appearance make her heartless? Again, the word shallow comes to mind. No, she decides. She was not put off by his size; the bond she believed would deepen with time was worth more to her than his physique. However, in hiding his age, there is no way to separate his photos from an act of dishonesty. Being Silky Maxwell is enough of a fabrication to maintain in her life. She doesn't want to consider what else he's deceived her with or think about what will come in the future if she fell for him and it was too late.

§

The app pings and she picks up her phone. "Thank you again for last night. You're one in a million."

"I had a nice time meeting you." She isn't sure what else to say. Her fingernails tap against her thigh. This would be the right time to mention going to a silent movie in Frederick if things had gone differently. It would also be the right time to bring up his photos. However, she's not angry. She has plenty of reasons for being Silky, and she is resigned to let him have his reasons for the photos.

"Are you free this weekend? Do you like sushi?"

She pauses. She won't go out with him again. "I don't think…" She deletes the words. Her fingernails tap the back of her phone. She's always shied away from confrontation. "I've got a lot of stuff coming up with work…" She deletes the words. The connection she felt has been severed, and it's painful to think of what could have been. She drops the phone into her lap. She doesn't have a good response. She taps, "You're a great guy, but I'm just looking for friends right now." This isn't true, but it's easy to say. Her finger hesitates, hovering over the small arrow to the right of her words. She exhales and presses it.

"That's the damnedest thing."

"What is?"

"I've met so many great women, you included. For some reason, everyone I develop a connection with is only looking for friends."

Her heart melts the way it does when she watches touching animal videos. The man she was attracted to was a great guy, a far better catch than Winston would have been. She questions her reaction. Was it the ultimate in shallow rejections, or were Hal's photos a fundamental act of deception? She chooses the latter so she can live with herself. She imagines this scene being replayed over and over for him. Her heart wrenches in her chest, thinking of all the women in her position, falling for an internet stranger, then meeting for the first time. None of us can tell the truth, she muses. She knows he wonders why mutual kinship and affinity peter out after the first date, every time.

She types, "It was nice getting to know you, Hal." Three dots appear a moment later. She closes the app. She rests her finger on it until it can be deleted. She taps, and it disappears from her screen.

§

Winter.

The photographer has done little more than nod at her since she arrived for the shoot. It feels too quiet in the studio. "Didn't you shoot the Luxe Precise campaign last spring?" she calls over.

"Yep," he responds, clipped and uninterested.

She walks over to him. "How does this look?" She runs her fingers over the fluffy, faux fur trim on her hat. She's wearing a corset and a pair of thigh-high boots, both trimmed in the same fur. "You'd look better without it," he answers without looking at her. He's adjusting the angle of the lights with his back turned.

"What's that supposed to mean?" She's put off by his comment. Sometimes, flirting with the photographer helps to channel the suggestive energy her photos are charged with. However, his comment was crude rather than the saucy banter she doesn't mind.

"I'm sorry," he says, turning to face her. "You're gorgeous, and the outfit looks great. I didn't mean you'd look better if you took it off. I—"

"What exactly did you mean?" She interrupts him. This isn't the way to begin a photoshoot, regardless of how much the brand is paying her.

"Let's start over. I'm Dean. We've got three hours and four wardrobe changes."

She's a professional, and this isn't the first time she's worked with someone who's spoken to her this way. "Got it, Dean. I'm ready when you are." She reclines on the fur rug, accentuating the impossible curve of the corset. Her fingertips rest on the fur around her cleavage. She parts her lacquered lips. Dean pauses, then presses the shutter. The lights flash. She shifts. He presses the shutter again.

§

"What was that all about, I'd look better without it?"

"I'm sorry. I know this is your job."

"It's not okay to talk to me like that."

"Okay, Silky Maxwell." His words are too cavalier for the conversation.

She doesn't raise her voice, but her tone is impatient. "You know what, Dean?"

"Hey, I'm sorry." He sets his camera on the table next to his gear bag and turns to face her. "This isn't going the way it should, and it's my fault. I'm talking about the way you came in with no makeup and your hair in a ponytail. Every day I see women in makeup and outfits like this." He motions toward her. "If I'm not shooting them, I'm editing them in Photoshop." He unscrews the lens from his camera and fits it back into a padded space in the bag.

They're eye to eye. She's still wearing the fourth wardrobe change, a black latex tube top as slender as a belt, a matching skirt with broad keyhole cutouts on the hips, and a towering pair of heels. She's still fully made up and in her signature black wig with bangs. "I don't see where this is going. What about my ponytail?"

"You and I both know this is a pretty sweet gig, but sometimes it gets to me. This is all made up." She flashes back to Winston. Even in her annoyance at Dean, she's glad he understands this is a job, not something distasteful. He continues. "When I edit your photos, I can make you a cup size larger with a few clicks. You're beautiful, but you'll never look as good as you will when I'm done editing."

"Nobody wants to see me in a ponytail, Dean. Where do you think I'd end up if I looked like that all the time?"

"I know. Where do you think I'd be if I didn't edit my work? It just gets to me sometimes." He pauses. "My dog died two days ago."

"I'm so sorry." Her hand covers her mouth. She doesn't expect a statement like that.

"I'm having a hard time seeing the point of this right now. I always wanted to be a nature photographer, like in Africa or the rainforest or something. Maybe shoot people's dogs on the side, but I know that sounds ridiculous. Gigs like this are what pays the bills so here I am. This morning I saw an ad from the county looking for a photographer to shoot portraits of shelter dogs. With my dog gone…" His voice trails off for a moment, and she does not interrupt him. "I mean, dogs are real, not like all this." He cocks his chin toward the set and the lights. "Does that make sense? Dogs know you. He was my best friend."

Ella sighs as a wave of understanding overtakes her.

"I get it. That makes sense. This thing I do is as fake as it gets. I've had a few things this year that really drove it home for me."

Dean is quiet. She waits for him to continue, but he doesn't respond.

She breaks the silence. "I know what you mean about looking better without the costume." She pauses. He is wrapping up a cable and fitting it into a slot in his bag. She thinks of feeling shallow after meeting Hal last fall. She's felt fake so many times since she nurtured being an influencer into a career. Dean is the first person she's met in the industry who's expressed disdain about the way they earn their living.

She watches him disassemble the lights. He isn't much taller than her, and they have similar coloring. He wears silver, wire-rim glasses, and it looks like he's skipped a few haircuts. He wears chunky black boots, and his jeans are rolled up to just below the tops of them. She watches him carry a light stand out of the studio. She wants to say something to call him back and draw him into a conversation. He disappears through the door before she thinks of something to say.

§

Ella turns onto Pennsylvania Avenue after leaving the shoot. Once she leaves the traffic of Washington, she can be at the beach in three hours. She's made this drive dozens of times and doesn't need her GPS. Pennsylvania Avenue will turn into Route 50, passing through Annapolis before transforming into a long stretch of flat, rural farming country. The muscle memory of driving without traffic lights and congestion has always helped her think. The winter seashore is gray and severe, far from a whimsical summer vacation. She needs a destination like this after meeting Dean. He's given her much to think about. She drives in silence and allows her mind to wander.

Dean countered Winston's hurtful words about what she does for money. He makes a tidy living photographing models and influencers and then erasing their flaws until they're more perfect than human. It's a job for both of them, and they both understand how it works. He also offset the loneliness that drew her to Hal by recognizing that their world is nothing but fakery, but there are people beneath the wigs and wardrobe. It still hurt to remember Cassie's stinging words that led her to the dating app, "Don't post that! Silky Maxwell doesn't bake pies."

She's right, Ella thinks. But I do.

She glances in the rearview mirror, changes lanes, and merges onto the shoulder. She scrolls through her email until she finds the one with the subject, "Call Sheet." Dean's number and email address are listed above the studio's address. Her heart begins to beat in her chest. She taps her fingernails against the back of her phone, then presses the digits. The voicemail answers after three rings. She fights an impulse to hang up. Instead, she begins speaking at the tone. "Hi Dean, this is Ella. Do you like apple pie?"

A Flame on the Ocean

The Anchor is crowded for a Wednesday afternoon. The men have been drinking whiskey, and Ruby has already tossed out two empty bottles. She feels protective of these men sitting shoulder to shoulder, each helping to drain the next bottle. They have arrived in Carrick Bend a little too early in the season. They've brought nothing useful to occupy themselves, save for wallets sufficiently filled to cover their bar tabs and rooming houses. In another week, these men will be at sea, and the bar will be quiet most afternoons. It is early summer, just shy of lobster season. It is also the beginning of hurricane season. This far north, these working men with rough hands, gruff voices, and beards to protect their faces from the wind, rarely consider hurricanes. This far north, they are reverent toward nor' easters, although they will have many weeks of sunshine and fresh breezes before the first boat will be lost in a gale.

She has opened The Anchor early and closed long after last call since the beginning of the month. She has been waiting for Tucker, far too distracted to clear cobwebs from the corners or polish the brass wall sconces that light the bar. She is glad no fights have broken out yet, believing any altercation before the season starts is a bad omen. Every time the massive wooden door swings open and light floods the gloaming interior, she stares at the silhouette. She wonders if Tucker has changed in a year. When the door closes, the shape coalesces into another lobsterman who sidles up to the bar and joins the others in drinking away his future paycheck. When the man who has taken a seat at the bar is not Tucker, her fingers rise to her throat in a Pavlovian motion to grasp a seabird-shaped pendant she does not take off. "As deep as the sea," is engraved on the back in a scrolling script as delicate as the motion of her fingers against the gold.

"You got Jameson, doll? I'll take a double," a man who has just entered calls out, taking a seat at the end of the bar. "Ruby, right?" A black knit stocking cap is pulled low on his brow. A smile forms on her lips before her gaze meets his. She is a fixture in this town, in this bar, a bottomless font of whiskey, bourbon, and ale. It seems that every man who has drank his fill in this bar remembers her. For many, her lips will bear the last smile they'll see before the steel hulls of their boats beat into the wind and cleave the waves as they lose sight of land. She cannot protect them from the moods and capricious whims of the elements. Instead, she can offer them another round, a tinkling laugh, and a honeyed voice that shares a story or insists they come back to see her when their run is over.

"Ruby, you remembered me," she responds, setting an empty heavy-bottomed rocks glass on the bar. Her pour is fluid and practiced, graceful against the dark, uneven sheen of the wood. He takes the glass with a hand bearing grimy half-moons of hardship under each fingernail. His knuckles are coarse and flaking, and letters spelling "risk" are tattooed on each finger. As he reaches to light a cigarette, she sees that the word "free" is tattooed on the fingers of his other hand. He is younger than her by a decade, but years older in spirit. He needs no words to tell a story of labor beaten into his countenance by harsh sun and wind, ice, and sea spray.

She carries the rote memories of tracing her tiny fingers over the bar's maze of carvings and cigarette burns as a child. "You've got the best seat in the house." She makes eye contact with the man, taps her fingernail on a small, smiling whale carved into the wood next to his glass. The letters BD are etched into the whale's belly.

"Who's BD?" he asks.

"Boby Dick. I was too young to pronounce the M, and my father thought Boby was just as good. Later on, I used to sit here to do my homework." Now, this man is no longer a stranger. She has let him into her world, connected him to BD and her history. He is unencumbered by family, roots, or obligations on land. However, once he arrives for the season from now on, she knows she will see him every day until he is called by the captain to ready his boat with the crew. She commits him to memory. She may be the only soul to remember him in future seasons. They share a private whale joke, and he will always look for a seat near BD on his return. Her father also carved small anchors, starfish, and mermaids into the expanse of wood for her amusement.

She has a story for each of these carvings, and another for almost every red wine stain and cigarette burn. She's cultivated many single-serving relationships with men set adrift who have no other ties to land, save for their claim to a seat at her bar. They will memorize the story she tells them while pouring their drinks. They will think of returning to that seat during long, cold midnight watches in which she is the only terrestrial beacon left to light their way into port. However, the stability of land and the choice to drink in a bar without the commitment to sweat, danger, and four-on, six-off watches will soon wear on them. They will pay their tabs and nod at her carvings. Then, back they will go toward the docks to gather with their crews, anxious to leave the safety of the harbor. Some are running away, and some are running toward, but the comforts of home do not figure into either equation.

There is a large, brass memorial plaque near the door, framed in warm oak, bordered with a thin, coarse braid of tan rope. "For the men and women of Carrick Bend who have been lost to the sea," is engraved at the top. Two centuries of names fill the bottom in three columns, with space for a tragic fourth on the right. She polishes the brass with reverence. Her rag always slows at the names of her father and his crew whose workboat went down trying to save a sailboat taking on water in a storm when she was nine. Men with grey beards and wrinkles radiating from their eyes from years of squinting at the sun across the sea have commented on the plaque. Many have shared their own stories of working men who did not return to land. She nods, refills their drinks, and wonders where their boat was on the night of her father's storm.

Most men who walk through The Anchor's door are familiar. Some, because of the stories she shared. Other men crewed on her father's workboat during lobster season. Others still knew her mother, a fixture behind The Anchor's bar before Ruby took her place. Each season she hopes they will retire before making the last run they may not return from. These men have seen waves as tall as city buildings. Few can say they've never borne witness to a careless member of their crew disappearing beneath roiling waves after being swept overboard. They are wise, salt-hardened in face and hand, and far more cautious than younger men who wear the fickle badge of invincibility like a maritime death sentence. Others, she climbed trees with and traded homework answers in school. She watched them grow taller, cultivate sparse adolescent beards and sinewy muscles, eager to follow their fathers down to the docks and out past the breakers.

Every time the shadow of a man looms in the doorway, and it is not Tucker, she knows the next one may be him. She has rubbed her thumb along her pendant's engraving more times than she is aware. She does not believe he would miss a season. She is patient. She will refill drinks and tell stories to her customers until the moment Tucker walks through her door. Alma, the old maid from her mother's sewing circle, has already offered to cover The Anchor when he arrives. Alma needs no more advanced notice than for Ruby to call across the street into Alma's open window. "Alma, he's here, can you come now?" will sound across the neat rows of snapdragons nestled in beds of pearl white crushed oyster shells. At this, Alma will wipe her hands on her apron. She will call back to Ruby that the canning's almost done, or the pie has twenty-five more minutes in the oven, or the roast is nearly ready.

Ruby fills and refills the bourbon, the beer, and the small wooden bowls of salted nuts that sit like sentries along the bar. In idle moments, she hums Tucker's song. She has known him for five years. Three years ago, he arrived to see her with a new guitar. Ever since, she has hummed his song to remember the words and melody, although she knows it would not be possible for her to forget. He confessed that he knew few chords but had mastered what mattered. They were on the couch in her apartment above The Anchor. She was sipping cherry brandy. Tucker's clear Jamaican rum was on the coffee table, strong enough to fell a draft horse. His guitar was propped on his knee. "Rum inspired song night, song number one." He paused. "First time ever." He looked at her, adjusted his fingers on the strings, began to pluck the chords. "I want to hold you, I hope you hold me too, I want to kiss you, I hope you kiss me too." He stopped plucking for a beat. He glanced at her, began to pluck again with confident fingers. "I want to love you, I hope you love me too." He drew out the final note and rested his hand on the guitar's neck. "That's the end."

The room felt warm. Ruby's chest fluttered. For a moment, she did not know whether to inhale or exhale. She moved her hand from her thigh to Tucker's cheek. His stubble, the color of winter wheat, was soft beneath her fingers. She brushed a faint scar on his cheekbone, thinking about Tucker turning down the wrong alley in a rough Newfoundland port. His eyes were a deep cornflower blue in the muted lamplight. "Yes," she said, "me too."

Every ten days between June and December, the lobster crews based in Carrick Bend return to port to empty the catch from their holds, stock their galleys, and fill their diesel tanks. On land between runs, they find brief comfort in whiskey bottles, hot showers, and the arms of women they love or women they pay to love. Each fleeting evening during this time for the last three seasons, she has listened to Tucker pluck the strings and ask for her love. She has fallen asleep in his arms every night that it has been possible. When Tucker's boat, the *Karen Bravo*, is filled with life at sea, Ruby comes alive, loves, and is loved in return. When the *Karen Bravo* is tied to the dock, and the deck is clean and quiet, her heart is also quiet. She waits for June. She hums Tucker's song to remember it for him. She believes he is humming his song to remember it for her as well.

Each time Tucker crooned, "I hope you love me too," she responded, "Yes, me too." The more he asked for her love, the closer she felt he was to leaving the *Karen Bravo* permanently at the end of a future lobster season. She envisioned the call and response of love and her affirmation were akin to building a port for him to call home. Here, she would have offered a permanent slip for the ship of longing and adventure he sailed. His pillow talk had often drifted toward whitecaps, spindrift, and the familiar sight of flying fish leaping from the sea. He occasionally spoke of vast, dry plains where one could drive for hours, passing only cattle and lonely oil derricks in their perpetual seesaw motion of newfound wealth. Once, he wrapped tendrils of her hair around his fingers and told her it looked like a bayou vine. He spoke of desolate mountain peaks that were snowy in the heat of summer. He whispered in her ear about murky, humid southern swamps, perennially shaded from the mid-day sun by verdant treetop canopies and thick, dense clouds of mosquitoes. Over the years, he sent few postcards, but she counted on one or two per year, using them as far-reaching mile markers to follow his journey.

When Tucker told her where he'd been or where he was going next, she considered each stop to be his last at that destination. She was satisfied that her inherited bar's income would support them both. The Anchor was always busy. Lobster season brought lobstermen. Autumn's tourist season brought camera-toting leaf peepers in search of lobster rolls in authentic New England harbor villages. In the off-season, townies filled The Anchor with the aroma of damp wool sweaters. She envisioned a golden ring to match the pendant Tucker had given her the year after he brought his guitar for the first time. After that, she dreamed of his retirement from the sea, hummed his song, waited for him to return to her for good.

§

Ruby comes up to the shoulders or the chins of the men who empty her bottles. Her features are feminine, yet strong and out of sync with her slight frame. She has said her eyes are blue to avoid explaining the central sunburst and the varied speckles whose colors change in the light. Her capable hands admit her strength without words. They are the hands of a laundress, a barmaid, a worker. They are red and chapped when The Anchor is busy, or dry and pink on her days off. Her hands are better suited to self-sufficiency and caretaking than to petting lapdogs and fingering the gossamer fabrics of party dresses.

In Carrick Bend, the women with soft hands accustomed to gentle pursuits are schoolgirls not yet assigned to their labors, or the wives of wealthy businessmen. She is neither. She knows no man worth his salt would take a wife unable to merge women's and men's responsibilities into one while her husband was at sea. She is a mirror image of many other women in many other towns along the New England coast; when the men are gone, they are a sisterhood, custodians of home and hearth. They turn the wheels that power the villages while their men tame the ocean's might and use the sextant and stars to guide themselves out to sea and away from the coastline.

§

"Well, it's Mickey Berring!" Ruby's eyes light up, and her smile is wide and genuine. It is just before last call, and the first of the *Karen Bravo's* crew has arrived in Carrick Bend. She is overwhelmed with relief. They have been friends since they were in third grade and Mickey's uncle was lost on the same rescue crew as her father. Once, Mickey took a man into the alley behind The Anchor who'd been fresh with her. When he returned, his knuckles were bloody. She never saw the other man again.

Mickey nods at her, smiling with his lips closed. She thinks of his missing tooth for a moment, glad Tucker was not on deck during last season's accident with the lobster pot. "Hey there, Ruby. How's it going?" She reaches down the long row of bottles to the Old Crow and pours him a double. Mickey is one of the few who will never have a tab at The Anchor as long as she is behind the bar.

"I haven't seen Tucker yet. Is he aboard?"

Mickey looks into his glass. His fingers begin to tap the bar, and it seems that he does not know what to do with his hands. "I'm sorry, Ruby. We just found out he's not coming this season. The captain heard he's on a whaling boat in the Faroe Islands."

"Whaling in the Faroes? When did this happen?" Her brow is knitted in disbelief.

"He's been on the *Bravo* a long time, but that's all the captain said. Wish I knew more." Mickey takes a large swallow of his drink and lifts his eyes to hers. She makes eye contact and nods, then turns away to refill drinks on the other end of the bar for last call. She needs to distance herself from the news her old friend has brought her before she falls into his arms and weeps.

§

The Anchor is now empty and quiet. She cannot remember Mickey leaving, what drinks she served since then, or locking the door after the last man got up from his stool. She believed she'd been focused on the autopilot motions of filling drinks and emptying ashtrays, a "just get through until closing time," sensation. However, alone in the still air of a bar that has defined her life, she realizes her focus has been little more than a dam. It breaks without warning, and the anguished torrent it releases is a rip tide, a storm surge she is unable to control. She wails, a long, high-pitched keening that the dark wooden beams would have struggled to support if her cries were made tangible.

She cannot identify the storm within her. Is it hurt, rage, betrayal? Her thoughts begin to swirl. The reasons for his absence form images in her mind that she is unable to put into words; a bar like The Anchor in another town, and a faceless woman who waits for him and fingers a chain around her neck; a fight after last call, a man who doesn't rise from the asphalt, and witnesses who can describe a knife in Tucker's hand, red and glinting in the streetlight. She allows her mind to go blank; it is too hurtful to speculate on his absence. Her palms slap the bar, out of time with her sobs. Tears pour down her cheeks. She clenches her fingers into fists, wanting to cause damage. The bar's surface is unyielding, and she finds no release. Her fist meets her thigh. The first impact is a dull, grey pain, palpable, a hurtful thing that gives voice to the eruption inside her. She beats her fists into her thighs, elbows flexing like pistons. She sobs and wails. Tears cloud her vision. She does not need to see to release this fiery, molten maelstrom into her beaten thighs.

Her sobs slow, stilling to dismal hiccoughs. Her thighs ache, and her head throbs. Her arms relax, and she releases her shoulders. She reaches beneath the bar for a napkin to wipe her face, and it comes away sodden. She inhales and exhales a deep, spent breath. She looks beyond the bar to The Anchor's tables, the aging, wooden beams, and the dark, heavy front door. The interior has not changed since she did her homework at the bar, but it is no longer the same place for her.

The silent television offers a bluish glow beneath an elaborate tangle of rabbit ears that nearly touches the ceiling. She turns off the VHF, tuned this evening to channel sixteen because the day's loop of maritime weather was unremarkable. She has little energy but forces herself to clean the ashtrays and wipe the bar. She does not sweep or mop, thankful The Anchor's regulars are accustomed to an occasionally sticky floor. There is a deep blackness in the pit of her stomach, an abyss that could not be filled with a late dinner or a shot of whiskey. She considers the sisterhood of women in Carrick Bend. The ways in which she is like these women are many; they share chores, they have perfected the art of waiting, and they wear jewelry from beloved men they believe will always return to them unless tragedy adds their name to The Anchor's memorial plaque.

The unique way in which she is unlike the sisterhood is now as plain as the affront of Tucker's absence; her necklace confirms little more than to say she has spent these years on hold. Somehow, Tucker did not share her vision of their future, or the radiance, warmth, and magic she felt during their time together. Instead, he has traded her love, her heart, and a home in Carrick Bend for the primal intensity of whaling in the Faroes. Her jaw and her fists are clenched, and she uses the back of one hand to wipe her eyes. She sometimes believed he would whisk her away from the burden of The Anchor with its mounting bills and growing list of needed repairs. Mostly, she believed he would settle there with her, and they would shoulder the weight together. She has another flash of the faceless woman who fingers a chain around her neck and waits for Tucker in another town. It does not fit the man she knows. There was no knife fight either. It is clear that he is wed to the enterprise of rootless vagabonding that an everlasting refuge made of wood, bricks, and Ruby herself does not permit. How stupid, she thinks, to have allowed herself to be a makeshift mistress to a man who is not coming home to her because she is not a home to him. She never considered the captivity a man with a spirit for flight would feel with merely a wedding band, a bar, and a tourist season to occupy himself with.

Before she climbs the stairs to her apartment to nestle herself beneath her mother's faded patchwork quilt, she tacks a note to Alma's front door. "Alma, he's not coming back. Can you open the bar in the morning?"

§

She falls into bed, but she cannot sleep. Her thoughts begin to twist from the sad emptiness of loss to blame and accusation. This misfortune is not her fault. She darts from herself to Tucker to The Anchor, looking for someone or something more guilty than the others. She settles on her parents, and her eyes fill with tears. How well-intentioned they must have been when she was a child, opening a bar to support a small family and supplement a lobsterman's wages. Her thoughts form sharp barbs of focus. It is easy to blame her father's valiant rescue efforts that sent his boat to the bottom of the sea. He abandoned a small child and a young wife with little skills save for cooking and tending bar. Her mother is next because her growing anger cannot stop with her father and his crew on the ocean floor. How dare her mother ignore a lump in her breast. How dare she leave a sixteen-year-old daughter a legacy, so fittingly called The Anchor. She utters something between a laugh and a sob, and her eyes fill with fresh tears. She thinks that The Anchor could just as easily have been called The Millstone, for all the burdens she has borne around her neck.

She cannot blame herself. She has always tried to do the right thing, feeling a responsibility to Carrick Bend's working men and women. The Anchor has been an anchor, a mooring ball and a safe harbor for working men with no other family. She has tried to fill that role for them, and for many years it fulfilled her. She considers the bar downstairs, and the men who have sat on its stools. It is hard to find much fulfillment in it now, with sore thighs, an ache in her throat, and few prospects for the future that are not grim, gray, and vacant.

On the morning of the second day, she lies in bed, staring at the ceiling. She feels less clouded, a little lighter. She brushes thoughts of blame from her mind. This is not about her parents. Instead, it is about a man who is whaling in the Faroe Islands, and how she chose to spend her time in the years before Mickey Berring's news. All those years were Tucker. Even yesterday was Tucker, but today is Ruby. Her pillow is still damp, and tears have glued her hair to her cheeks. She climbs out of bed, pulling the offending strands away from her face and weaving them into the rest of her hair with her fingers. The apartment is silent. In the bathroom, she splashes cold water on her face, avoiding the mirror. There is no need to inspect herself for puffy eyes, dark circles, and skin that is likely pale and blotched with red.

She thinks of the note she tacked to Alma's door. Kind Alma left comfort food at Ruby's door while she was in bed, but Ruby placed it uneaten in her refrigerator. She is ravenous for it now and heads to the kitchen. Alma came with pie when Ruby's father and most of the town's best men failed to return to land. When Ruby was sixteen and her mother passed, Alma came with steaming casseroles and chunky, buttery chowders. She stepped into the dual role of barmaid and mother so Ruby could finish school. Alma will open The Anchor on time for as many days as Ruby needs her to. She will pour the beer and flirt with the greybeards like a schoolgirl. She will tell her own saucy stories about the carvings on the bar, but she will close it at suppertime. At her age, even Alma has her limits. Yesterday as the sun crossed the sky, Ruby wept for her loss. This morning, her throat and sides ache. Her thighs feel bruised. There are four slender crescent shapes pressed into each palm, and she cannot eke out another sob. She begins to consider that Tucker is not a great force that has blindsided her with malice. Instead, she closes her eyes and strips herself of emotion. She examines what has galvanized his spirit, what she failed to realize about him.

The words she held closest to her breast, "I want to love you, I hope you love me too," no longer hold a promise for the future. As though the clouds have parted to reveal a divine truth, she understands that Tucker's song was genuine in the moments he sang it to her. However, his words extended promises no further than that of waking up together for the next sunrise. She cannot offer Tucker the experiences of the vast, dry plains. She does not know what swims beneath the surface of the brackish water in the bayous and swamps. Was he there last spring, or spring a decade ago? She has subsisted on trinkets of little value, crumbs of attention, three lines of a song. He did not promise her more than those lines. She did not think to ask him for more, and only assumed herself into a permanence with him. Many seasons of her life have been dictated not by promises and guarantees of a future together, but by the *Karen Bravo's* schedule during lobster season.

The shadows have lengthened, and the light has changed. She puts the kettle on for tea. The last five years are now as clear to her as the church bells from St. Olivet on the hill. The fault of this monstrous misunderstanding falls not on Tucker, but on her alone. Without realizing it, she cherished him for the places he'd been and the myriad reasons he hadn't remained in any of them. She knows she could not love a man who didn't long for exploration or the feel of a rolling deck beneath his feet. She knows she could not wholly desire a man whose ambitions included nothing more than helping to manage The Anchor, or eating lobster caught by another man. When they were apart, Tucker was illuminated in her imagination like a flame on the ocean. This, she knows, cannot be contained within four walls of a dingy seaport bar.

Carrick Bend and her own embrace were pins on Tucker's map, she reflects. He has moved on. What was once a welcoming destination is now a memory for him to cherish or to forget. Her assumptions toward their future together mimicked a captivity Tucker's heart could not allow. She failed to consider the imprisonment he would feel with Carrick Bend and The Anchor as his final destinations. Whaling in the Faroes, she muses; instead of settling with her, he's sailed across the sea to pursue the novelty of traditions not his own for the sake of excitement. Instead of dining on another man's hard-earned catch, he lives among those who herd pods of pilot whales into the shallows to feed the villages. They are not even his villages, she thinks indignantly. Now, he wades savagely into the water with local men, pulls the disoriented whales to shore with hooks and ropes. Now, he stands among long, black slaughtered shapes in waves that lap the shores, salty and deeply crimson with blood.

Tucker is not coming. Who is she without her attachment to him? Aside from a shabby legacy that now weighs heavily upon her, what else is left in Carrick Bend? She eats Alma's stew and sips tea from the last unchipped teacup from her mother's old set of china. She is pleased with the clarity beginning to settle over her. She breathes in, considers the woman she will become if her future does not include a life with Tucker. She breathes out, begins to make plans.

§

She stands before the bathroom mirror, hair gathered in one hand. Her mother's good quilting shears are in the other. She severs the hank in two satisfying snips, drops the dismembered locks that Tucker loved so much into the small wicker trash can between the toilet and the sink. The remaining hair brushes her shoulders and will never be mistaken for a bayou vine. She tucks the shortened ends behind her ears and considers that there is much work to be done.

She thinks of Alma, of Grace, of Esther, and Amelia, the dear widows and spinster aunts of Carrick Bend. She is childless and nearing middle age where people will begin to think of her as one of them. To stay in this town, obligated to tend bar until her hair goes to silver would surely set her on a spinster's path. She has no interest in women's gossip, putting up beets and cod for the winter, or sewing circles. She glances in the mirror again, deciding that any new lines on her face should come from a sun that does not shine upon a lobster town this far north. Tucker spoke of plains and long, straight highways, mountains, and swamps. She knows only the northern coastal sky and the familiar sea with its whitecaps and steely grey waves. Inland, she has only seen the gently rolling New England hills, wooden covered bridges, and the splashy grandeur of autumn leaves. It never occurred to her that she might also see a mountain peak topped with snow in the heat of August. For all the years of her life, her history has been as firmly entrenched in Carrick Bend as its Puritan founders. Today, her hair is in the trash and Tucker is not coming back.

The sun has set. She turns on a lamp, surveys her two-room apartment. For the first time, the rooms seem too small. The furnishings appear to have grown overnight, crowding the space. The air begins to feel stale and hot. She opens a window, but it does nothing to release the constricting feeling that has settled over the space. Almost every item is heavy with nostalgia, and she feels the weight settle onto her skin like a heavy blanket. The rooms are filled with things representing moments in her life that she fears she wouldn't be able to recall without them. Her mother made the floral curtains as she watched at seven, legs too short to reach the sewing machine foot pedal from her seat. There is the patchwork quilt on her bed. Her mother's ashes lie in a wooden box on a rosewood side table next to a frame displaying two Navy medals from her father's days as a young sailor. She has clothing, books, and her mother's wedding ring, which she slips onto her finger. She has no pets, and there is little else of actual value in these rooms.

There is one bottle of Jamaican overproof rum in the cabinet over the humming refrigerator. She does not drink it but keeps it for Tucker. She smiles but is quickly serious again, thinking that she needs it far more than he will. She pulls her father's ancient olive drab seabag from the top shelf of her closet and packs her purse, toiletries, and a few changes of clothing. She leaves space on one end of the bag for the rubber-banded bundles of cash she saved in a small safe in the kitchen crawlspace. Her mother became mistrustful of banks after her father died. Ruby continued using the crawlspace after her mother's passing, getting money orders at the post office for everything that could not be paid in cash. She glances at her watch. Carrick Bend is asleep at this hour. The bars have long closed, and the streets are empty. Working men and women do not burn the midnight oil in towns like this.

§

She pulls Tucker's rum from the cabinet and hefts her father's seabag over her shoulder. She makes no sound as she pads down the stairs and enters The Anchor, although she has no reason to be quiet. Alma lives across the street, but there are no neighbors on this side. She sets the seabag on the floor in front of the bar's weighty wooden entrance door, uncorks the bottle, inhales the familiar scent of Tucker. She is not nostalgic. Instead, she is ready for the new dawn that will follow this purge.

She weighs her decision. She has made a grave mistake with her affections. The Anchor once felt like a comfort she could call home. Now, it is little more than a support to others, and a tether for her. The Anchor is a dingy, dive bar without Tucker. It caters to a clientele attracted to a place where the liquor is cheap and the lights are dim. The men, many who have seen the world's ports, take comfort in being served by a barmaid who is unchanged, season after season. She pictures dropping dead behind the bar, but at least the lobstermen's drinks would have been refilled before she expired.

She has never been out west. The widows of Carrick Bend have never been there either. Years and husbands have passed for them and whether they once cared or not has been long forgotten. If she is to stay at The Anchor, to be weighed down by the crushing load of the actual anchor the bar has become, she knows she will no longer care either. When the sun rises in a few hours, Carrick Bend will hold nothing but countless bleak and identical seasons of men passing through, but none staying. She opens the bottle, drops the cork to the floor, hesitates. She tips the bottle and a small puddle forms at her feet. Nothing happens. She is motionless. This can still be undone.

It is not too late to set the bottle on the bar. She could tack another note to Alma's door asking her to take over while she sorts things out. She could drive through the Appalachian mountains, find a westbound interstate in Pennsylvania, and make the rest up as she drove. She knows Alma would relish the chance to step in. However, she also knows she'd eventually point her car east again. She'd settle back into The Anchor's rhythms in her too-small apartment filled with her parent's remnants. She'd wait for Mickey Berring's seasonal greeting and tell stories to traveling men about the carvings on the bar for the rest of her days. Mickey and his crew could make their home in any port, but she'd be forever beholden to Carrick Bend. She does not know how to proceed, other than by removing the possibility of The Anchor shackling her further.

She splashes rum on the floor as she paces to each of

the most substantial support beams. She flings the bottle haphazardly to cover them and the adjacent walls with liquid. A feeling of anticipation rises in her chest. She is light on her feet, splattering walls and tables. She splashes the aged, decorative monkey's fist knots that hang from the rafters, the roughly hewn, knotted planks of the floor, and finally, the wooden bar with its stories of her girlhood. The iron pot belly stoves on each end of the room are cold and empty. She leaves them dry, knowing they will survive this. She has emptied the bottle and sets it down carefully. She unclasps the chain from her neck without touching the seabird and drops it to the floor. What was once the freedom of a bird in flight now seems to be an albatross that no longer has a place around her neck. She plucks a matchbook from a bowl behind the bar, slings her bag over her shoulder, and walks toward the door. She glances at the plaque that bears her father's name, and her heart catches. It belongs to The Anchor, not to her or any new, false home she could place it in. She strikes one match, holds it toward the book. Her face glows orange as the book catches with a hiss.

She tosses the matches into the first puddle she made. It ignites. A channel of flame moves toward the beams at a startling measure. As the fire licks the first beam, luminous offshoots find the walls. She imagines this new, fleeting network of ignition looks similar to the bayou vines she has never seen, but she has no desire to observe the rest of the combustion. She opens the door and steps into the fresh night air. Her car is parked in the gravel lot behind the bar, and she sees that the flames are not yet visible from outside. The Anchor has no windows, so the bonfire glow will only appear as it devours her second-floor apartment. By that time, her car will be just another vehicle on the long and lonely interstate.

§

The low radio melds into the lull of the road. Her mind is clear. However, aside from the pull of the cardinal direction, west, her destination is not. She has never seen Boston, Chicago, or St. Louis. She is curious about the towering mountains that dwarf the Appalachians, the vast plains she'll pass through, and sunsets that color the sky like a rosy watercolor painting and dip into the ocean. She feels no regrets for wanting to become someone new. She knows Alma will forgive her.

Her mind wanders to the multitudes of nearshore and offshore boats that have left Carrick Bend's harbor to begin the season. That is all she has ever known. There are men on night watches on each of those boats. They are cold, solitary, watching the stars, watching for lights, watching for other boats. She knows that on a boat at night, the rolling sea and the dome of the sky appear to merge into one, and the boundary of land is sometimes difficult to discern at a distance. She wonders if The Anchor's pyre will be visible to those men on deck, illuminated like a flame on the ocean.

The Geography of Flight

Tess threw her apartment key out the window on I-95 North. What was there to go back to? In her mind, Mercy Cove shone brighter than a lodestar. She felt a pull toward Maine, instinctive, magnetic, migratory. She set the cruise control and settled into the rhythms of traffic. The first few hours on the road passed quickly, and she allowed her mind to wander. This endeavor held the newness of possibilities, escape, and reinvention. At the very least, the job at Mercy Cove was in an isolated location with nobody to ask about her face: How did it happen? Does it still hurt? How long will it take to heal? Did he ever get caught?

The GPS chimed at the Georgia state line, and she glanced at the remaining mileage north. She thought less about how far she was from Mercy Cove, and more about these things: how far she was from the apartment for which she no longer had the key, how far she was from the woman she'd been when she occupied the apartment, and how far she was from the little girl who first learned about the opportunity a hurricane could bring when you needed it the most.

§

Mercy Cove felt like a blessing, allowing her to vanish and slip into the life of someone new when she needed it. Her mother's long-ago logic stated that humanitarian aid after a disaster should be there for the taking if only you wanted a fresh start.

Tess knew the hurricane that destroyed Garland Bay was not truly manna from heaven, but what choice did she have? She now wore an angry, uneven autograph from a man whose rage had altered her identity. Tess Before was her mother's daughter; far more stunning than girl-next-door pretty. She wielded a perfected smile-and-take attitude so deftly that she wanted for nothing. She aged in the way of women accustomed to being a wealthy man's trophy, creeping from beauty toward elegant sophistication. Tess After was no longer even a pretty face. Her scar brought pity and aversion, things that did not pay the rent or fill the cupboards. She'd never held a job that did not depend upon her appearance, and she had no idea how else to make her way in the world.

When Tess was in elementary school, a similarly destructive storm demolished Port Anthony on the Gulf Coast, half a day's drive from their home on the outskirts of Memphis. Tess's mother bundled her into the car shortly after the waters receded and spread a map over her lap. There was a fat line drawn in one of Tess's markers leading from their neighborhood on the eastern bank of the Mississippi River toward the gulf. "Get us there, Tessie," her mother said as they merged onto I-55 South.

"What about my books, mama?"

"We'll find someone else to buy you books." Her mother rolled the window down slightly, lit a cigarette, and announced that the storm was a gift from God. In Memphis, her mother's generous heartbreak smile had earned her the best cocktail shifts and the worst kind of boyfriends. She alternated between smoky nightclubs and vicious tempers until the time she could not go to work because of a black eye that makeup could not conceal. The same day, a hurricane in the Gulf of Mexico made landfall. Shortly after that, Tess sat in the front seat with a map spread over her lap. She counted down exits and practiced ways to say they'd lost everything in the storm surge.

Tess and her mother arrived on the coast amid the cleanup. They sussed out the church group most likely to offer charity to a clumsy single mother with an accidental shiner. A compassionate do-gooding couple put them up in a spare room. The husband was kind to Tess. As a child, she thought of him often, never having seen a husband and wife existing peacefully in a house together outside of television.

Within a few days, Tess's mother had fabricated a resume more impressive than her spotty work history slinging beer and Keno cards in a pair of cheap high heels. On the new resume, she spent a decade at the cosmetic counter of a local department store that went out of business. She listed her most recent job as a home health aide for an elderly client who passed away. Now here they were, returned to town amidst the aftermath with nowhere else to go. "It's just my luck," her mother sighed as the volunteers presented her with job openings and apartment listings. "We've come home, but now home is gone. What am I going to do with Tessie when school starts?"

Smile-and-take: they were given a basement apartment rent-free, "Just until you two get back on your feet, hon." Smile-and-take: the charity group found Tess's mother a job in a church administrative office. Smile-and-take: Tess's mother's new boyfriend bought her a fur coat and an emerald necklace, her birthstone. He often had riddles and small, tough rectangles of pink bubble gum wrapped in a miniature comic for Tess. She smiled at him, learning smile-and-take before she could articulate the concept. Later, he split her mother's bottom lip and put his fist through the wall. The following day, Tess found herself in the front seat with a map on her lap again.

“Get us there, Tessie,” were her mother’s only words for miles. They’d moved many times. She knew there would be pretty things for her mother, and books and trinkets for herself in the next town.

§

When Tess’s mother died unexpectedly, Tess identified the body with one soft-spoken syllable. She took the bus back to their weekly-rate motel, sandwiched between a pawnshop above a liquor store, and a Chinese-fried chicken-submarine sandwich carryout. She searched the room for her mother’s diamond earrings, a gift from a long-ago man who had been kind. The earrings were not on the nightstand or in the large, velvet-lined mahogany box where her mother kept gifts she chose not to pawn each time they moved. Her mother must have been wearing them.

For the first time, at seventeen, Tess needed her own plan. Aside from the box, the room held nothing else of value. Her mother’s lifeless body had been found in the nude, sexually assaulted and beaten almost beyond recognition. They’d had an unspoken agreement in the way of plans and who made them. Her mother kept them fed, rented hotel rooms by the week, and made sure Tess did not have to use the soft prettiness she had grown into as any form of currency. In return, Tess asked nothing of her mother on the long drives with a map on her lap. She never questioned her mother’s bruises, new jewelry, designer handbags, or shopping sprees. Her mother said little on the road. Instead, she hummed along with the radio and took slow, deep drags on her Virginia Slims.

Tess sat on the bed in the weekly rental. A neighbor

flushed the toilet, and the pipes knocked. A car door slammed in the parking lot. She inhaled her mother's faint, fading perfume. Her mother had been nude countless times, and she had been beaten often enough. It was unthinkable to imagine an occasion when neither would happen again. But that occasion was now, today. Tess was alone with a box on her lap that the pawnshop could convert into many more nights in this weekly rental, to groceries, to time.

Inside her room, she wanted the dance of the hours to slow. Outside her room, cars would continue to drive. Women like her mother would continue to take what they could from men in an endless loop. Men like those her mother knew would continue to offer kindness and dinner dates, or hands and mouths that did not stop until they found what they were seeking. Here is the cycle, a vicious inheritance passed down from her grandmother to her mother, and then to her: You are a commodity to sell. Find an easy mark. Give of yourself, but not everything. Deplete, drain, squeeze, but do not fleece. We are not that kind of women. The men, orbiting in hand-me-down cycles of their own, became their fathers: Hands gripped tight into fists, or hands with fingers flexed, and palms flattened, slicing through the air. Goddammit woman, you're pushing me again. Objects thrown. Objects broken. I didn't mean it. Second chances wrapped in loving words and small boxes. I'll never do it again.

Four hours later, Tess stood unapologetically in the pawnshop with her mother's mahogany box. She pawned everything, including the box. The perspiring clerk with a long, oily ponytail passed a stack of bills to her over a glass case filled with engagement rings and gaudy gold watches. She did not count the bills as she stuffed them into her purse. She left the pawnshop, walked without direction for an hour. For the first time in her life, no one expected her home. Her mother had been fine until she was not, but in the way of the young and invincible, "until she was not," would never factor into Tess's equation. She knew her mother's routine with men by rote, but it had not occurred to her until now to mimic it.

It was in this way that Tess got her own pair of diamond earrings from a man who did not leave her bruised. Later, there was a slender tennis bracelet from a man who did. She learned to walk effortlessly in her mother's sky-high heels. Initially, she was surprised when men confirmed that she was no longer the gangly, awkward girl she'd been during puberty. The power she held surprised her as well, this new influence over adult men, many old enough to be her father.

Seasons passed. Hurts were inflicted. Wounds healed. Sometimes, there was joy. Every New Year's Eve, she wore a sparkling new dress. There was always a new man to press his lips to hers as the ball dropped, and whisper that she was the most beautiful woman at the party. There was someone new by springtime and always another to keep her warm as the seasons changed. There was another still to kiss her at midnight as the new year commenced. In this way, the surprise of her power eventually faded, replaced with expectation and need.

Tess ate well, drank little, and never smoked because it was bad for the skin. She drifted through cities, relationships, and injuries both tangible and imaginary. She searched for a man like the do-gooder volunteer from her childhood hurricane escape. He was real. She believed there were others like him, and she would give up everything if she found one. She identified him in strangers too quickly and loved these mistakes fiercely. She left them without warning when the letters in the words, "I love you," transformed from warm embraces into something sharp, and dark, and bleeding.

She volunteered at the animal shelter when she had time, preferring toy breeds and lapdogs. She buried her face into the fur of strange animals as she crooned love songs to them. With these warm balls of abandoned fur in her arms, she did not feel alone in the world. She followed her mother's advice, delivered once when she was thirteen while watching her mother prepare for a date: Don't cut your hair. Wear sunblock every day. Splash with cold water at the end every time you wash your face to tighten your pores. Always sleep with a satin pillowcase to prevent wrinkles. Tess applied expensive skin creams at night, and SPF 100 to her face and hands during the day, even when it was cloudy. Along these lines, Tess moved from girlish beauty to mature elegance with ease. There was always an older man looking for a trophy, a woman to make them look better as their waists spread and their wives aged before their eyes.

§

She had known two ways to live. Neither suited her now. Tess Before was taught that everything she wanted was hers. She had only to meet the right man and decide how much of herself to offer up. Sometimes what she offered was everything, with little to show but debasement in return. Other times, she offered hardly more than a sliver and was richly rewarded. The scale rarely balanced in an obvious way. Sometimes loneliness tipped it far out of balance. These times, she'd sooner sell herself to the lowest bidder for an empty, lustful smile and a glittering trinket than allow loneliness to overtake her again.

Most men she knew were wrong for her. Eventually, she encountered the most wrong of wrong men. In quiet moments since that night, it was not difficult for her to remember the vivid silver glint grasped in his hand, as much a weapon as it was an eraser of her very self. The pain was a blinding flash of heat lightning in the blackness of a summer night sky. Tess Before vanished. She was replaced by Tess After, a stranger. It was impossible to accept the fragility of her identity, but the ache on her cheek, the blood, and the mirror were a murderer's row of certainty. Without warning, she was no longer fluent in the language of taking, the something-for-nothing vernacular bequeathed by her mother. Tess Before, trapped in the breathtaking cruelty of Tess After, could hardly navigate this new permanence. Then, the hurricane struck.

§

Alone in her apartment, she read the news on her laptop: ".... unprecedented strength this early in the season… new normal in climate science…" She fingered the wound on her cheek without thinking. She stopped answering her phone. She watched news clips of faraway seaside locals boarding up windows. She tried yoga, made an effort to adopt a new centered, deep-breathing persona. The Governor of Florida declared a state of emergency. The disaster porn on her newsfeed flashed with dire warnings, landfall predictions, mandatory evacuation orders. She had not left the house in three days.

She did not have a mahogany box on her lap. Instead, she had a scar. People shared clips on social media of fronds being ripped from Garland Bay's palm trees. Meteorologists urgently counted out the rising storm surge measurements. She followed the rescue efforts. She reread old novels before bed. The storm weakened, moved up the coast and out to sea. FEMA was praised for arriving early. She baked cookies, ate them over the trash can until she felt sick, threw the rest away. Coverage slowed in the 24-hour news cycle. She scrolled and clicked out of habit, pausing at an article about an upcoming job fair for Garland Bay residents who wanted to relocate, rather than rebuild. She wanted both of those things for herself and noted the job fair's date and time. She heard her mother's whispered voice. The storm was a gift from God.

§

The shadows were lengthening when Tess stopped the car at a gas station with one pump. A dusty stuffed black bear with cloudy glass eyes, bald spots, and two missing front teeth guarded the store's entrance. "Hi, this is Tess MacKenna. I'm at Mick's Stop n' Gas. They said to call from here." The elderly ranger on the other end provided concise, easy directions: *take a right out of the parking lot, look for the sign, take a left, keep going when you think you've gone too far, can't miss it.* She wrote the directions on a small notepad, ended the call, and tucked her phone into the glovebox. She'd been told the signal past town was spotty without MaineTel service, and there was no one else to call.

§

The land surrounding the cottage was designated as a protected bird sanctuary, home to countless species of native and migratory birds. The sanctuary contained a mature spruce forest, acres of saltwater marshes, and miles of deserted, rocky coastline. Tess would live in the old keeper's cottage and make daily rounds, observing the birds and their nests. The ranger she spoke to on the phone was waiting for her at the cottage. They toured the grounds, and he provided guidance for recording her observations. He reminded her three times about the instructional binders in the cottage. One was for the birds, and the other outlined the simple acts of living at the sanctuary. He chuckled when she asked what a composting toilet was, but his humor was kind.

§

She reviewed the binders on her first night. The bird binder outlined the observation procedures; what to look for, how to collect and record the data, and how to submit it. It cautioned against getting too close to the birds and their nests and advised the observer never to interfere with common springtime squabbles over mates and territory. She did not cry when she read this binder.

The cottage binder described an alien, off-grid world. She wept in defeat as she turned the pages. How could she live without indoor plumbing? Electricity came from a solar panel on the roof. On their tour, the ranger showed her how to operate the generator just in case. He assured her the panel would keep the small refrigerator running if she used the oil lamps at night on cloudy days. She imagined forgetting a critical step, running out of matches for the oil lamps, spending many nights in total darkness. The composting toilet needed to be emptied regularly. In her first week, she mopped up her own carelessly overflowed waste more than once. She was humiliated that her life had been reduced to cleaning a spilled toilet. With the scar, she believed she would never be elevated to more than this new, useless version of herself.

On her third day, she awoke to dark skies and a downpour. By lunchtime, she thought of the solar panel and the food in her refrigerator. An hour later, she was soaked to the skin and still trying to start the generator. She burst into tears and kicked it forcefully. Her rain boots were a cheerful yellow plaid, flimsy and stylish. When her toe made impact she burst into tears, crying out the word, "Fuck!" many times until her throat was sore.

She often cried in her first few days. She could only manage to heat her bathwater to lukewarm or boiling. She had yet to master the stovetop coffee percolator. There was no microwave. Twice, she sat in her car sobbing, key in the ignition. Was it harder to stay at the cottage and live like she was camping, or leave Mercy Cove and drive to a place she could not name? Both times, Mercy Cove won. She could not convince herself to drive into the sunset because she knew night would fall. Where would that leave her? Mercy Cove was at least a job, a place to live, and plenty of time to feel sorry for herself.

In the cottage, drinking water came from five-gallon jugs, stored in a large pantry closet. The binder listed the grocery store in town as the drop-off point for the empties and recommended the quantity she should return with on every trip. Rain barrels provided water for bathing. The water had to be heated in a large, dented pot on the propane stove and poured into a tub. She was left to figure out which of her moisturizing body washes, anti-aging facial cleansers, and costly hair emollients worked best in rainwater. How defeated she felt, remembering the empowering seductiveness of the salon and the cosmetics counter. When she wallowed in the perceived ruination of Tess Before, she reminded herself that someone had taken almost everything from her, but not her long, silken hair. She brushed it with a handmade British boar-bristle brush, maintaining the nightly ritual she'd seen her mother do.

Did the cottage's hardships make up a better life than the unknowns she would have encountered if she stayed in her apartment and tried to make do with her new face? How would she pay the rent with a scar? She accepted this position blindly, but to what end? It was hard not to vacillate between trying to be grateful for the solitude, and longing for a life she could no longer lead. She pressed her fingers to her cheek and pitied herself, unable to stop thinking of restaurants with cloth napkins and elegant stemware, or expertly maneuvering her limbs in a Pilates studio without breaking a sweat.

It took a few days for her to notice the natural light that filtered into the cozy, one-room cottage. Sheer, gauzy curtains covered the windows. The walls were painted a pale, creamy shade of yellow that softened and warmed the atmosphere. A portly potbelly stove sat in the corner next to a large, empty wrought iron wood holder waiting to be filled with firewood. The cottage smelled of the sea, an organic aroma that strengthened when the sound of the surf drifted in on the breeze through the open windows.

An oversized canvas watercolor hung on the wall opposite the couch. It showed variegated swaths in shades from dawn's lightest watery blue to the deep, rich ochre of the salt marsh. An elongated flock of wavy black lines soared high within the blue. Small, scrolling letters at the bottom read, "The Geography of Flight - CCB." Sometimes she pondered it in the evenings before bed. It was soothing and might have been a homecoming if Mercy Cove had not felt like such a foreign world. She wondered if the artist had lived in the cottage, and how long it took them to feel at home there.

Adjacent to the dated but functional kitchenette sat a worn wooden dining table for two. The couch converted into a large, comfortable bed. The velvety, blue blanket thrown over the back of the couch matched one of the watercolor's stripes. Although the days were warm, the evenings this far north were cool. Tess took comfort in curling up under the blanket with a dog-eared book from the tall shelves adjacent to the front door. The selection included volumes on New England's native bird species, an Audubon Society ornithology field guide, a pristine Gideon's bible, and every issue of National Geographic from 1967 to 1980. The library also contained the beginning half of a set of Encyclopedia Britannica ending at K, westerns and true crime stories, thick, sweeping romances, and Coastal Cooking's Best Seafood Recipes. A few pages of the cookbook were spotted and stained, and page 109 had been torn out. A handwritten recipe for spruce needle tea was tucked inside the front cover. She read it twice, repositioning it like a bookmark to remind herself about it later.

In the beginning, Tess took to the mirror after breakfast in an attempt to feel normal. She could not let go of her previous identity's cosmetic bag rituals. She tried to be eager to greet the birds and delve into her observations and tasks, but she could not break habits that were still a part of her. Her instinct dictated that she should be ready to impress a new stranger at any time. She needed these tenets to exist as herself, these aesthetically pleasing foundational tropes that had filled her wallet and emptied her spirit. There was not another soul for miles, and nobody would notice whether she penciled in her brows, but it did not occur to her to skip it. She struggled to keep her manicure from chipping as she traipsed through the forest in search of nests and flocks. She carried a tube of lip gloss in her pocket at all times. She could not keep up with the routine her long hair required. It became a halo of disappointing, unmanageable frizz, despite her handmade brush. Sensible ponytails made her scalp ache by mid-afternoon, and she felt helpless at the decline of something so integral to her former life.

§

A month after she arrived at Mercy Cove, she drove past Mick's Stop n' Gas to a strip mall. She parked her car and fought the urge to back out of the parking space and merge onto I-95. Head south, or veer west when she hit Boston? She had no idea. Instead, she sat in the parking lot, trying to still her anxiety and define herself in light of this shopping trip.

Mercy Cove's influence, the very notes of its scent and flavor, were like nothing she'd experienced. The personal effects, cosmetics, and outfits she brought were so useless that they were a hindrance rather than a benefit. But these were the things that defined her. Her hands were developing calluses, her nails were broken, and her hair was a frizzy tangle. She was unable to make her old accouterments work in this new place, but she did not yet identify with the items on her shopping list. However, necessity forced her to at least try them on.

She purchased sports bras, work boots, and sturdy clothing from Walmart, much of it thick, brown, and flannel. She also bought a pink plastic comb, unscented, healing hand cream in a utilitarian tube, unscented white bar soap, and lip balm with added sunblock. It felt like she was shopping for a disguise or a stranger, her twin in size but foreign in comportment and personality. She glanced at the cashier but kept her head turned to the side. The new items were more suited to the wildlands than the leisurely, flattering collection of tight jeans, push-up bras, and ballet flats she'd been struggling with.

Tess did not bother with the pretense of inflated confidence among women. Her eyes welled with tears as she entered a brightly lit discount salon with many open seats. She had her acrylic fingernails removed and the polish stripped from her toes, all without making eye contact with the nail technician. She could have kept the ponytail, but to what end? The stylist chewed gum with the same vigor she employed to close the scissors over the thick hanks of hair in her hands. Tess thought of retiring her boar-bristle brush for the comb and could not bring herself to glance at the dull mound on the floor as she paid and left the salon. The sensation of air on her neck and ears was unexpected. In the car, she reached to grasp her phantom hair, but her fingers closed in on themselves.

An unfamiliar inclination crept into her periphery. It was not until she was in the tub two days later, washing her new, pragmatic haircut, that she was able to identify it. The feeling was relief. She was surprised and hesitant, realizing she'd transformed into someone she did not recognize. This was not Tess After, an empty shell previously occupied by Tess Before. This was something new and unrecognizable. Could it be that this was simply Tess, neither a before nor an after version, just the new Tess that she had become?

In Mercy Cove, settling into a routine dictated by the birds, the land, and the weather came easily once she was mentally and physically equipped for it. The new boots felt like large, constricting blocks around her ankles. Soon, she came to appreciate their sturdiness when she could no longer feel every twig and stone beneath her feet. She was grateful for the ample utility pockets in her new pants, and she began carrying snacks and small, useful implements into the forest on her walks. Once, she nearly stepped on a thin black snake coiled in her path, much more like a shoelace than a predator. It slithered away from her boot, and she laughed out loud. She would have screamed and ran in her ballet flats, a virtual lifetime ago. She would not even have been in the woods in that lifetime. However, here she was in her new normal, with protective boots and a meaningful reason to be in the spruce forest.

Twice a day, Tess wandered the property with a notebook and a pair of scuffed binoculars she found in a drawer. Her knowledge of bird behavior was limited to the cottage's reference books, but that did not deter her. She took to the endeavor with a deep focus formerly reserved for securing a dinner date on nights in her youth when her wallet and her cupboard were equally bare. She sat in the forest for hours, listening to the chirping, trilling chorus set against the surf's crashing rhythms. She observed the flocks from a distance, watched for patterns, began to notice how the birds and vegetation in Mercy Cove appeared to work seamlessly together.

The spruce did not crowd each other within the forest. Each tree had enough space to spread its branches. The towering trees that rose into the canopy did not cluster or bully their smaller neighbors out of space. The saplings sprouted and matured to the exact height the surrounding forest could support. Every tree's reach was impeccably suited for it alone, and the entirety of the timberland existed in harmony.

There were marsh birds and forest birds who called to their flocks in unique, musical chirrups. They pecked, hopped, roosted, and soared. Their movements appeared haphazard until she'd spent hours observing them. Each bird knew where to find its meals, how to build a nest, and where to seek shelter. The invisible magic of instinct drove the flocks into the sky in a blur of feathers and beaks. Other times, flocks in flight glided down from the sky in silent synchronicity, each landing in precisely the right spot. The flocks roosted in the trees or nestled in the tall marsh grasses where they were difficult to see. They took flight, landed, and rose into the sky again. The shorebirds were her favorites. They possessed an instinct to dip their narrow beaks into the wet sand when it was safe and flee the breakers when it was not.

The spruce forest was always in motion, as were the birds and the marsh. This was not a performance that paused when Tess retreated to the cabin in the evening. Mercy Cove continued its cycles, perfectly in sync, and her body fell into step. She became accustomed to the cottage. She observed, she read, and she slept deeply without pills for the first time. Her daily agenda and sense of purpose had nothing to do with her appearance. Some days, she forgot about her scar. Her brief morning and evening rituals no longer required the mirror, so she removed it from the bathroom wall.

§

Tess taught herself simple maintenance tasks in the

long evenings after dinner. She found a thick, orange hardback DIY manual from a big box hardware store in the shed. The shed also contained tools and equipment she had no previous experience with, but she was a quick and curious study with plenty of free time. Soon, there were no squeaky hinges in the cottage, and the table did not wobble. She climbed to the roof and secured the solar panel that rocked in heavy winds. Hammers were the domain of men, but Mercy Cove had blurred the line between pink jobs and blue jobs. Successfully using tools in an unfamiliar way brought satisfaction that working to receive diamonds never had. This coincided with the fulfillment she felt after completing complicated repairs, and a formerly damaged thing worked like new. She was grateful for a new way to define herself.

Tess's first set of observations received perplexing comments: "Excellent work, you're a natural! Please continue in this style." She had not spoken to another person since her last visit to town over two weeks ago, but she spoke the words, "excellent work," aloud with brio. No one had ever said that to her. Mercy Cove was not work. She fell into a fit of giggles, repeating the words in various authoritarian accents. Work was paying the rent in ways she was not proud of. Work was permitting a first date's hand to creep from her knee toward her thigh. Work was living as the manifestation of her mother's endowment, rather than relying on a paycheck's stability. Birds were not work. Strolling beneath the towering spruce with a notebook and a pen was not work. Listening to the wind in the boughs, smelling the aromas of the coastline, and sleeping alone every night was not work. The formerly irksome off-grid cottage was no longer work, either. Nothing about her existence in Maine was work. Nonetheless, she was being praised.

She stopped thinking about where she'd go when she left. Instead, when turned into if; if she left, but why would she? What was there for her past Mick's Stop n' Gas and the strip mall? It had been so onerous to occupy her own skin in the beginning when she sat in her apartment alone, fingering her scar and binging on cookies. She hadn't looked in the mirror in weeks, but somehow, she had succeeded admirably in sturdy boots and tough utility pants. At the same time, she'd begun to forge the steel of her insides into another shape. A new shape, a new person, the woman she was destined to be. She could not have done this with the coquettish tools available to Tess Before. In the evenings, she studied the painting hanging on the wall opposite the couch, and she finally knew how long it had taken the artist to call Mercy Cove a home.

The Box

The mailman dropped a stack of envelopes and a rectangular box wrapped in brown paper on the counter. His forehead was beaded with sweat from the mid-summer heat. He gave Jessie a perfunctory nod, paced across the lobby, and shoved the door open in an explosion of tinkling bells that hung from the door. Jessie picked up the box, letting the envelopes fall to the desk. It felt too heavy for its size, a solid, weighty shape whose contents did not move when Jessie shook it. Her name, care of The Bel Alton Motel, was written in her younger sister Crystal's childish rounded blend of script and print. There was no return address. The stamps were crooked, mismatched and overlapping, in contrast to the sharp corners and the paper's straight edges. Jessie imagined her sister cutting a grocery bag along the folds, laying the box in the center, creasing the corners like origami. Once the box was wrapped, she must have been overtaken with a great urgency to be rid of it.

§

Jessie shook the box again and replaced it on the raised counter, next to the silver bell and warped, plastic "Please ring for service!" placard. The air in the lobby was warm and still, and often retained the odor of cigarette breath long after the smoker had breezed back into the parking lot. The counter's dull yellow and white surface was webbed so evenly with timeworn hairline cracks that they appeared deliberate. The shabby, maroon carpet was worn to black in places, and threadbare with patches of grey plastic backing peeking through in others. A chain attached to the counter that had once held a pen dangled over the edge. Business at The Bel Alton Motel, formerly one of Maryland's finest mid-century motor courts, had declined when the interstate highway was built. The Bel Alton and a scant few others in the area remained open during the following slow decades, catering to down-at-the-heels travelers and salesmen with trunks full of door-to-door wares.

The bells on the lobby door tinkled again. A man entered and strode toward the counter. Jessie straightened, smiled out of habit, watched him slap a fat, ruddy palm onto the silver bell before she could greet him. His pale yellow dress shirt was unbuttoned at the neck, with broad, translucent circles of sweat beneath his arms. A faded red Hoover Vacuum patch was embroidered on the pocket. "I'm ringing the bell, and here you are. How's that for service?" The man's grin was wide and affable, ready to befriend her and begin a sales pitch. His forehead shone with beads of sweat, and his cheeks were flushed. "Hot enough out there for ya?"

Jessie's expression was polite, but she did not engage him. She broke eye contact and moved her sister's box to the desk below the counter. She did not need to know this man to know his kind. "Welcome to The Bel Alton, sir. How many nights will you be staying?" Any more conversation than necessary with The Bel Alton's clientele and they'd inevitably ask if she knew a place where a man could get a good hamburger in this town, what time she got off, or if she'd accepted Jesus Christ as her personal savior. She'd completed this check-in hundreds of times. She knew this man would ask for one room for one night and she'd assign him a room near the vending machine.

She'd dangle his key by the oval plastic keychain so he could take it without touching her hand. She knew he'd glance at the room number embossed in chipped gold ink before exiting. She knew he'd leave a rumpled bed and towels on the floor. The maids would find an empty bottle or two, a sticky plastic cup on the nightstand, and an ice bucket filled with lukewarm water when the ice machine was working. Occasionally, the maids would discover a trash can filled with vomit or a trail of dark droplets on the carpet leading to a bloody hand towel in the sink.

The man who rang her bell took the key for one room, one night. He glanced at the room number on the keychain, 12, and departed to the clamor of bells. As the door closed, he called, "Thank you kindly," over his shoulder. Jessie was alone with the box.

§

Jessie and Crystal did not exchange birthday gifts or Christmas cards. Jessie could not remember receiving so much as a postcard from her sister. As adults, only a few years apart in age, they barely knew each other. Their last communication had not gone well, and they hadn't spoken in a few months. Jessie expected to make the first move toward mending the fences once she allowed Crystal's embers to cool. This unlikely gift was out of character, but Jessie was glad Crystal had reached out. Jessie remembered Crystal hissing into the phone during their last call, "He's waiting for you." Her vehement insistence seemed to come from nowhere. Alternately, Jessie disbelieved that she alone was responsible for giving a comatose, dying man, a stranger to Jessie, permission to depart.

"He's not waiting for me, Crystal. It doesn't work that

way. Our father's dying. There's nothing else going on." Jessie's tone was even, a cool splash of water sent through the telephone line in an attempt to diffuse Crystal's fire.

Crystal spat her response, verbally grappling for control. "There's no other reason he'd be hanging on except that he's waiting for you. How can you let him suffer?" Crystal insisted that Jessie leave work immediately and drive from Maryland to Florida without stopping. Did Crystal intend that she arrive at their father's bedside as a guardian angel instead of a guest? Crystal wanted the upper hand in anything she could grasp. However, Jessie could not fathom how Crystal determined that the tenuous balance of their father's final moments depended on Jessie's arrival. Jessie was a foreign, forgotten lifetime ago to this man, not a beacon of release to guide him into a tunnel of ethereal light. Crystal longed for an imagined past while Jessie looked toward a future of her own making. When Jessie found out Crystal had played detective and located their father a few years prior, she did not even bother to feign interest. What satisfaction could come from asking someone who'd stepped out of your life without looking back to suddenly take on a starring role?

Jessie ended the conversation with her sister, unwilling to accept this fabricated encumbrance. Why hadn't Crystal celebrated this responsibility, playing the hero while cradling their father's frail hands in hers? Surely, she had the right words for this man she didn't know, a blend of, "You're free to pass on," and, "I always loved you the most." If nothing else, Crystal was skilled at conceiving of attachments and constructing them from barely more than wisps of memory and faded photographs.

In three decades, Jessie had seen their father twice, yet, she did not feel a loss or the need to create a family from nothing. When Jessie was fourteen, she visited their father and his second wife for a long weekend. He taught her how to identify his instrument, the bass guitar, by playing the old Creedence Clearwater Revival song, "Have You Ever Seen the Rain?" He tapped out the bass on his thigh with his fingers, repeated dun dun… dun dun… with the chords. She'd been a quick study, tapping in unison into the chorus and refrain. As an adult, she was not sentimental about the time spent with her father, but she could not listen to that song without hearing the instrument as clearly as the vocals.

She called his house at eighteen, in need of an abortion and grasping at straws. His wife dismissed her with the name of a bar where her father's band was performing the following evening. Jessie and her boyfriend begged gas money from a roommate and made the seven-hour drive. She watched him on stage in his faded jeans, cowboy boots, and large brass belt buckle. She kept time with his nodding head and his tapping foot and identified the dun dun… dun dun… that his fingers drew from the strings. When the band took a break, she told him why she'd come. He offered nothing more than two sodas purchased on the band's tab. Jessie and her boyfriend did not stay to see the second set, and her boyfriend stole the money from his parents the following day. She was grateful for someone who had more regard for his aversion to fatherhood than he had for stealing from his family.

When Jessie and Crystal were small, Jessie's mother juggled relationships. She did not want to be alone and could not pay the rent by herself. Jessie, intelligent, strong-willed and bold, absorbed the alternating rage and unwelcome attention of her mother's flings. Crystal avoided the men, playing with dolls in the safety of their shared bedroom. Jessie's mother drank cheap wine and chain-smoked cigarettes. She insisted the attention was Jessie's fault for sassing and dressing like that. Rather than staying to become a target for something physical, she had run away at twelve and entered the foster care system shortly after. Crystal stayed, becoming a solitary bull's-eye in Jessie's absence. She shouldered the burden of wreckage and hardship alone, setting her at a disadvantage against Jessie's years of stable, indifferent foster homes. Now this, Crystal's insistence that an absentee bassist who'd offered Jessie a soda but nothing to Crystal ever, was critical, immediate, and Jessie's problem to solve.

Fatherless daughters were a dime a dozen and Jessie was thankful not to share the experiences of other women. Too many fathers and father figures caused more damage by staying than by walking away. Before Crystal located their father, she had not seen him since she lost her first baby tooth, but Jessie was not surprised at her sudden performance as a caretaker in his time of need. Crystal must have relished the contrived sense of belonging, allowing herself to feel like someone's daughter. Jessie did not need similar inventions. Instead, she filled the holes in her life with a different man who gave her a permanent record, rather than a family.

§

"This shift has been pretty uneventful. No families, no single women. Keep an eye on seventeen, though. I've heard the door slam one too many times. Millie left a batch of cookies in the back, and that's pretty much it." Jessie gave Mitchell, the night clerk who looked like a grandfather from a Norman Rockwell painting, the perfunctory shift change report. She handed him the master key ring as she prepared to leave. Mitchell had been working nights at The Bel Alton since Clinton was president. Although overnight check-ins or partiers were rare, Mitchell was adept at sizing people up. He knew when to say there was no vacancy, despite the empty parking lot. The Bel Alton's third front desk clerk, Millie, was plump, dependable, and eager to please, and the three of them ran The Bel Alton Motel's front desk without error or incident.

Mitchell looked at the box in Jessie's hand. "What's that there?" he asked as Jessie walked toward the door. She was impatient to end her shift and shrugged her shoulders slightly, rather than offering an explanation. With little to do overnight but doze and nip on the bottle of gin hidden in his pocket, Mitchell relished bits of gossip from his coworkers. The choicest morsels came from the maids, but Jessie had failed to provide anything more than what was required at their shift change. She found a refuge at The Bel Alton Motel when she was sure no one else would hire her, and it had provided a fresh start when she needed it the most. Although Mitchell was a kindly old drunk, he was not a friend

"It's not much, a gift from my sister," Jessie responded and opened the door. A fresh gust of summer air blew into the lobby. She was looking forward to sleeping in the following morning. She had the next two days off and did not want to waste any of it on Mitchell. "I'll see you later."

§

The box felt heavy in Jessie's hands as she crossed the parking lot to her cottage. The cottage had been the honeymoon suite before The Bel Alton's decline. However, when the "No" on the vacancy sign was never lit again, the owners removed the mirror from the cottage ceiling. They replaced the burgundy velvet blackout drapes with coarse, beige curtains, and offered the cottage to an employee willing to accept reduced wages in exchange for a place to live. The previous clerk had eloped unexpectedly, and the owners were desperate for a pretty face to work at the drab front desk. Jessie was the right person at the right time. They had not asked about her work history when she applied for the job with a warm, eager smile. She had not needed to translate shelving books in the women's correctional institution library into job skills in her interview, and she gladly accepted the front desk position. The previous clerk left the cottage full of worn but useful housewares and faded area rugs to cover the discolored linoleum floor. Jessie was also pleased to discover a few drawers of cast off, out-of-style clothing which all fit well enough with a few alterations and a belt.

Although she was glad for The Bel Alton's front desk smock to wear over her second-hand clothing, she did not care to be fashionable. The Bel Alton Motel was a fresh start, and she was pleased to be a single, anonymous front desk clerk. This new, invented life came without a past. She was no longer a lost girl turned into a lost woman. She no longer loved the wrong man. In her reinvention, she would not make grave mistakes born of bad judgment and a desperation to be wanted by someone. At The Bel Alton, Jessie was polite, diligent, and meticulous. Her cottage was neat and orderly. She had rekindled her relationship with Crystal and saved enough to buy a used car with one headlight, two balding tires, and a working engine.

When she checked single, attractive women into the

motel, she gave them rooms in the back where their foot traffic would not disturb the other guests. These regulars were polite, quiet, and never left messes for the housekeeping staff. They were indebted to Jessie for providing them a safe place to earn a living and feed their children or their habits without judgment, out of view of the county police. The irony that shelving dogeared novels in a canvas prison jumpsuit had kept her from joining their ranks was not lost on her.

§

Crystal's brown-wrapped box must be a peace offering, an olive branch. It brought Jessie comfort, knowing her sister wanted to apologize badly enough to mail a gift. Crystal had been so unreasonable, insisting that Jessie could ease their father's death, and Jessie was proud of her for wanting to make amends. She was surprised Crystal hadn't merely called. However, neither had the tools or the habits of apology bred into close siblings. As Jessie slid a paring knife through the evenly aligned strips of tape, she thought of calling Crystal in the morning to say hello. Their mother had disappeared while Jessie was incarcerated, likely run off with another musician, and Jessie had no one else to call.

The brown paper fell away to reveal a cardboard cigar box and a folded white piece of paper. *Primo del Rey Fine Cigars* encircled an unimpressive red and gold foil seal. Jessie unfolded the paper and read the note in confusion. "Your turn," was written in Crystal's plump handwriting. She turned the note over, hoping for an explanation. It was blank. The words, an unusual way to apologize, meant nothing. Jessie paused, momentarily forgetting to open the box. She recounted their last conversation, Crystal's seething insistence, and the guilt she tried and failed, to inflict like a wound. Jessie placed the note on the round, wooden table, raised the box's lid, and furrowed her brow. The box contained a clear plastic bag filled with a light grey, powdery substance. She untwisted the bag's loosely tied knot, curious as to why her sister would send her a bag of… dirt? Dust? Ashes?

Jessie dropped the bag into the box, filled with the electricity of a sudden shock. Ashes from her sister in a hastily mailed box with no return address. A note reading, "Your turn," following their father's recent passing. This was not an apology at all. Instead, this was an affront, a slap across the miles to deliver a sting a telephone call could not accomplish.

Jessie inhaled deeply, exhaling slowly and relaxing her shoulders. Her heart was pounding. Her hands shook. The wall she had built to separate herself from the scores of abandoned daughters who grew into damaged women was collapsing. She braced herself for the earthquake of emotion whose epicenter sat immobile and grey before her. Her eyes began to prick with tears. She pushed the box toward the center of the table. She would not permit any part of herself to fall into the open bag, commingle with the ashes of a man who had never been there for her. Yet, here he was in a sickening reversal of roles where Jessie was the caretaker. Her father, now innocent, absolved of sin and relieved of worldly pain, waited for her next move in his cheap, cardboard cigar box, in her cheap, one-room cottage.

§

The cottage was immaculate and sanitized. In Jessie's

two days off, she had pilfered industrial cleaners and solvents from the maid's closet and thrown herself into scouring the cottage. Her back was sore. Her fingernails were broken. The only surface that remained untouched was the kitchen table. She'd been unable to do more than turn her back to it and keep moving, scrubbing, and bleaching until her eyes stung. Every time she sat down to catch her breath, the box seemed to grow. Its needful aura expanded to occupy her small home, and her father was there. He filled the air with his absence and presence, and everything that duality had represented throughout her life. His invisible specter, the ghosts of her own making, and Crystal's words, "Your turn," fought for Jessie's attention. She fought back. She scarcely slept, purging the cottage of dirt and disorder with fierce, frenetic energy. Jessie was determined to keep the looming, disagreeable manifestation at bay as it threatened to unearth every shortcoming of her upbringing. When there was nothing more to scrub than permanent stains, her energy waned. She was spent more from the battle in her head than from what she'd cleaned and sanitized.

§

Crystal's phone rang and rang. Jessie did not know what she would say when Crystal answered, and she was not sure how long she listened to the hollow tone repeat itself. She returned the phone to its cradle on the wall. It was probably no longer even Crystal's number. She sat at the table and looked directly at the box, weary and sore from her efforts to still its explosive existence. During her fury, she'd begun to let a creeping idea for self-preservation filter into the edges of her thoughts. She stared at the box, considering both the role reversal it presented and where she was going from here.

§

On the third day, Jessie stepped into the lobby, giving a small wave to Millie who was behind the desk. "Oh, honey, are you okay? What happened?" Jessie had not bothered to wash her face or change out of yesterday's filthy jeans. Her hair was barely in a ponytail, with the strands in front hanging in her face in disarray. She had eaten little and could not remember brushing her teeth last. She looked worse than she felt, knowing the drama of her unexpected dishevelment would work to her advantage.

"I have… I have a family thing. Can you and Mitchell cover my shifts? I'll be back as soon as I can. I need…"

Millie interrupted. "My God, Jessie, take as much time as you want," Her expression was sincere and concerned. She leaned over the counter to squeeze Jessie's shoulders in a compassionate gesture. Jessie was glad she hadn't bothered to fix her hair as she walked from her cottage to the lobby.

"Thank you, Millie. I'm so sorry about the short notice, it's just that…"

"You look a mess, girl. Get yourself in the shower and don't come back until you've sorted this out with your family. We'll be fine here." Jessie's eyes welled with tears of gratitude. Millie would have been this kind even without the unkempt appearance. "Now, you go on," Millie scolded gently. Jessie nodded, wiped her eyes with the back of one fist, and stepped into the sunshine.

§

Jessie's secondhand, leatherette suitcase was packed and sitting next to the door. The hot shower had eased her aching muscles and brought her clarity. She'd kept her head down after being released from the correctional institution. After her release, she shed her canvas uniform like a cocoon, emerging into freedom as a new person comprised solely of her life at The Bel Alton Motel. Her dubious, occasional relationship with Crystal was as superficial as neighbors talking over a hedge. Reminiscing about a childhood together that ended when Crystal was eight and Jessie was twelve only carried their conversations so far. Jessie's childhood defiance made her a more convenient target than her sister. However, at twelve, she did not have the forethought to predict what running away would do to Crystal. She had not been there to protect a tiny, freckled eight-year-old with long, strawberry-blond pigtails.

That freckled child could not be blamed for growing into a spiteful, bitter adult who saw Jessie as having all the advantages because she held a steady job and owned a working vehicle. When the hospice nurse pronounced their father dead, Jessie imagined Crystal losing the false control she'd concocted. Her pretend family was shattered, and she'd dropped this into Jessie's lap maliciously. Crystal liked having the last word, and there were few statements more final or vindictive than, "Your turn," accompanying a box of ashes with no return address.

§

Jessie did not plan to travel aimlessly. Her destination had come to her during a fit of back-and-forth scrubbing in which she wore down the sponge and split two fingernails to the quick. She left the cottage at sunrise, spent the night in a motel west of Nashville, and rose before dawn the following morning. The box loomed on her front seat. During the long stretches of rural road when her car was far from other traffic, she fought the urge to force her foot down on the gas pedal and throw the box from the window. She wept three times but pulled over only once when she sobbed too hard to keep her car in the center of her lane. She did not move the box to the back seat, mistrustful about what monstrous shape it might take if she could not see it at all times.

At the Oklahoma state line, she bought a map at a truck stop. She asked the cashier about the reservation north of Tulsa, and they carefully outlined the route in black pen. She hadn't known Oklahoma was her destination until it came to her, but it made so much sense. She knew three things about her father's childhood, but only one of them was accurate. She was sure her father's father had built and restored antique player pianos somewhere near the state line. The other two were romantic deceptions her father had courted her mother with when their relationship progressed from bassist and band groupie to an engagement. The first tale was that an unnamed ancestor rode with Jesse James. The second was that the contrived stagecoach robber married an Osage Indian and settled on an Oklahoma reservation. As the only identifiable location in her father's fanciful history, the reservation's open landscape appealed to her more than searching the state for vintage player pianos.

The highway turned into a long, flat straightaway, humming under Jessie's tires. The radio marked the hours, alternating between static, twanging country, and sermons that filled the car with the commanding enthusiasm of hellfire and tithing. The air blowing in through the open windows whipped her hair around her face like a halo. She glanced at the map before slowing to take her exit. The rutted, two-lane road was bordered by power lines, stubby trees, and rolling grasslands that blended into greens and ambers. There were few houses or buildings, and no other vehicles on the road. Short of the far-flung idea of reaching Oklahoma with a cigar box full of ashes, she had not planned this. She had no idea whether to scatter them, bury them in the ground, or bring them home with her again.

In the distance, Jessie could see a flashing red railroad crossing light. A long train stretched across the horizon. As she approached, it was apparent the train was not moving. She slowed to a stop, grateful for the interruption and unsure she was even ready to reach her destination. Nonetheless, she understood that whatever occurred on the reservation beyond this crossing held great importance.

The train was motionless. Jessie scanned its length but could not clearly discern the caboose from the engine. She turned her car off and stepped out to stretch her legs. She had been few things to fewer people. At The Bel Alton Motel, she had done small favors to help the working women, and she'd fed an occasional colony of feral cats when the kittens were born every spring. However, she had failed her own sister with no regard for the damage until recently. She had been a burden to her mother, interrupting her drinking and smoking, and continuously driving her mother's companions into a rage with her insolence. She had been merely a good time, and later a driver and lookout for the boyfriend who didn't want to be a father. She'd loved him as desperately as she wanted him to love her in return. She had been inconsequential to the man in the box, but what could she be to him now? She was bringing him home, and whether the romantic stories about Oklahoma were true or false no longer mattered.

The wind was still, the train was silent, and Jessie was alone with the ashes. She glanced along the train's length a second time. At one end of the train, she saw two uniformed figures carrying toolboxes. They disappeared between two cars. She stared in that direction for many minutes, but they did not reemerge.

She got back into her car, reclined the seat, and gazed into the cloudless blue sky. A large, dark bird circled overhead. More arrived, and shortly, there were seven circling in flight. She watched their wings tilt slowly, rising and falling with the updrafts. These birds were carrion eaters. Something nearby was dead or dying. Soon, they would swoop to the ground to make a meal of whatever creature they were stalking. The birds continued to circle the car, occasionally swooping low over the roof. She could hear them calling to each other with cries that sounded like "why..." The birds called, circled, called. Jessie watched.

A bird landed on the car's hood. Jessie did not move as it extended its wings fully, stretched either for balance or a warning. She glanced up to see the rest of the flock circling low, calling "why… why… why..." The bird on the hood hopped forward, stared at her with its small, black, unblinking eyes. It had a long, curved beak, sharp claws, and leathery, black legs. "Why… why… why..." continued to sound above the car. The bird's head shot forward without warning, beak connecting with the windshield in a mighty smack. She sat up, heart pounding. The bird took flight without a sound.

"Carrion eaters," she thought. "I have the dead thing in here with me." She looked at the car's interior, the maps, and the box as though seeing them for the first time. These things belonged to her, but she did not belong to them. She had cobbled the damaged, delicate pieces of herself into something of great strength, but she had crumbled at a small, cardboard cigar box. She had permitted it to own her momentarily, allowed it to compel her toward a state she had no reason otherwise to visit. "I'm done," she spoke aloud, glancing from the box to the train. "I'm done with this."

She was nothing to the dry, inert ashes. Oklahoma's relevance ceased to exist as Crystal held their father's lifeless hand and the hospice nurses came in for the last time. Her father's affection or acceptance would not materialize from the ether beyond this stationary train. At twelve, she could never have saved Crystal from their mother's blind eyes. Had she stayed around to try, she would have ended up far more flawed and broken than any of the women at The Bel Alton or in the correctional institution. This sojourn would not offer her redemption from the choices a twelve-year-old child made. She had never felt more certain or lucid.

Jessie saw an open boxcar three cars down from the crossing. She paused, straining her ears for the sound of machinery or the railroad workers she'd seen. The train, the birds, and the grasses were hushed. She grasped the box and stepped out of her car. Gravel crunched beneath her feet as she approached the boxcar. She did not look inside as she set the box down and slid it away from the opening. She turned away from the train and looked into the sky. The circling, calling birds had disappeared. A breeze lifted her hair from her shoulders, and she inhaled deeply. She closed her eyes and let the cleansing wind wash over her. Her guilt and shame fell away, replaced in the gust with crystalline brightness. She felt lighter, luxuriating in the release granted by the birds.

She slid into the driver's seat and started the car. She did not pause to look back at the train as she turned the wheel into a U-turn. She pressed her foot on the gas, enjoying the rush of wind on her face. She turned off the radio when the static merged with a bellowing preacher, castigating sinners who could not be saved. She did not need the voice of an evangelizer to know that she had saved herself, with a little help from a train that had not moved, and a flock of black, circling birds that had.

Truck Stop

On Saturday morning, Caro begins the drive to the Outer Banks listening to a novel. She cannot concentrate on it, so she turns it off and drives in silence. With the ring two days gone on another highway, she could be any single woman on southbound I-95. A shiny, blue convertible with Florida plates passes her, and the driver's hair catches her attention. A platinum blonde ponytail whips in the wind, gathered through the elastic of a powder blue baseball cap. Caro does not like the sun and breeze that come with the top down, but she considers the type of woman who does. Maybe this woman prefers hiking or volleyball to theater tickets. Could Caro learn to enjoy sunbathing on a Florida beach? Her eyes follow the convertible as it accelerates, then she watches a silver minivan change lanes ahead of her. There are two stickers on the bumper: "My child is an honor roll student at Tucker Middle School" and "Go Tucker Tigers!" Caro does not know what middle-schoolers are like, but she could probably get used to it, especially with an honor roll student. She wonders if this one likes to read books, and imagines herself as the mother of a tween.

A black, mud-spotted pickup truck passes the minivan. The back window holds a sticker of a twelve-point buck's head, and another of a large, green-and-white fish curled into a semi-circle. She can see the outline of a man driving. A woman with curly hair sits next to him. Caro pictures herself in the woman's place, imagines reaching over to hold the driver's hand. They probably have a woodstove and a neat pile of split wood that he chops in early fall when it is still pleasant enough to leave the windows open.

She puts herself into every vehicle near her, confident that none are on their way to a honeymoon alone. She presses her ring finger forward, unconsciously moving her thumb toward it to spin the diamond band of her engagement ring. Her finger is bare, and the space feels deserted. She has no plan for how to spend her time when she arrives at the beach house, or who to become when the reservation ends. Her own life is in pieces, useless and virtually stamped with the word "counterfeit."

Everyone traveling in her direction seems to have a destination with solid pillars holding up a roof they can live their lives under. Caro, on the other hand, has neither a satisfying destination, a semblance of pillars, or even the idea of what kind of life she will go home to.

§

Monday's pedicure seemed like weeks ago when she'd looked up from the phone in her lap with wide eyes. She felt the nail polish brush splash past her toenail and onto her toe. She must have jerked her foot when the text came in. She stared straight ahead, and it felt unnatural, this gaze toward nowhere with brimming eyes. If she blinked, tears would spill down her cheeks. If she kept her eyes open, they would not. How long could she go without blinking? Maybe until the pools dried, or until this moment became imaginary, the text disappeared, and she went back to work with toes painted in Manhattan Red. Maybe the week would continue as planned, or perhaps it would not.

Thick, icy liquid seemed to spread from her stomach into her chest but her skin felt hot. She was unable to hold the phone steady with her trembling hands. The pedicurist sang out a musical annoyance in another language to the pedicurist at the next station, then she looked at Caro. Their eyes locked. Caro could not help herself, and she blinked. Tears spilled down both cheeks. The pedicurist's grip on Caro's foot relaxed, and both women lowered their eyes. The pedicurist gave Caro's foot a gentle squeeze, but neither looked up again. Caro looked at the phone on her lap but the letters in the text message were blurred.

It was Monday during Caro's lunch break. Her wedding was this coming Saturday. The expansive seating chart, all calligraphy and flourishes, leaned against the bedroom wall at home. Little white favor boxes filled with dark chocolate hazelnut truffles sat in rows, covering the entire dining room table. The uniform green bows on each box faced the same way, and Caro had taken care to line up the polka dots on the ribbon when she assembled them. Her wedding dress hung on the closet door in a clear zippered garment bag. During the year-long engagement, she had an intricate tattoo on her back of thorny brambles and crimson roses removed so she could confidently wear the strapless mermaid silhouette in front of the Wheatleys, Evan's prominent and wealthy family. The mandatory last-minute meetings and appointments were scheduled like puzzle pieces.

She called it a dream wedding because she liked the sound of the phrase. It felt like the right label to characterize the wants of a girl she had not been, and a woman whose attributes she'd molded herself into in order to become. It almost felt brazen to free herself from the coarse, destitute habits of her childhood and own the desire for a life with someone like Evan. A dream wedding did not ring true in the dark place where formative memories dictated she should slump into the cycles she fought against repeating. However, she had succeeded, earning the right to be a woman with dreams that included more than making bail for an on-again-off-again boyfriend, or budgeting the benefits check so there was still enough to eat at the end of the month.

She blinked from her perch in the pedicure chair, wiped her eyes with her fingertips, and reread Evan's text: "I'm not doing the wedding. Cancel it."

§

She came home from work enraged and fumbled with her key in the lock. It almost bent in a moment of panic when she imagined that the lock was changed instead of sticking as usual. She flung the door open and stomped into the living room, prepared to release a string of barbs beginning with how preposterous it was to cancel a wedding by text message. She stopped when she saw that Evan's computer desk in the corner was bare, and she approached in disbelief, as though the computer would materialize with a closer look. Instead, there were only the dusty outlines of the monitor and keyboard and many faint water rings above the smudged silhouette of the mousepad.

She stood in front of the desk and tapped his entry on her speed dial, but the voicemail answered during the second ring. She imagined him fumbling for his phone and accidentally sending it to voicemail, and she tapped his entry again. It went to voicemail on the first ring, erasing the momentary hope that he'd tried to answer her call. She listened to the automated greeting, not even a human voice she could try to draw meaning from. She could guess at the reasons for his absence, both from the apartment and also when he disappeared into his computer every evening, but none were satisfactory. Hadn't she cultivated herself into the type of woman Evan preferred, the very person the Wheatleys wanted for their son?

She walked into the bedroom. The top of his dresser was empty, and she did not bother to open his drawers or peer into his closet. His toothbrush was not in the bathroom. His deodorant was not in place beside her nighttime retinol serum. She returned to the living room and collapsed onto the couch, envisioning him carrying his belongings to his BMW in haste, checking his watch often to ensure that he pulled away before she got home. Her rage and panic at the sticky key felt like the fading echo of an explosion, something more deflated than destructive. She stood and walked toward the dining room table, covered with a festive green and white army of celebration favors. She gathered as many as she could hold in one arm and tossed them onto the couch. She brought a bottle of wine, a corkscrew, and a wine glass from the kitchen, and sat down among the boxes. Her throat tightened as she tore one open without untying the ribbon, and the tears began to fall as she put the first truffle into her mouth.

§

At eleven o'clock on Thursday morning, Caro's department manager called her into the conference room. She saw that everyone in the office was already gathered around the large, polished mahogany table. Each corner of the bright, airy room was filled with silver and green balloons. Green and white streamers were taped to the walls, and a set of silver crepe paper wedding bells hung from the ceiling. A large white sheet cake sat in the middle of the table, decorated with a filigree of sugared flowers. A stack of green plates, forks, and napkins sat next to the cake. She had come back to work on Monday without mentioning the pedicure; there was no corporate jargon to explain becoming an unplanned, "it happened to me," story at the salon.

The room erupted into a cacophony of joyous voices when she entered, and she forced a radiant bride-to-be mask to spread across her face. Someone cut the cake, and a plate and fork appeared in her hands. Her coworkers hugged and congratulated her. She returned their hugs and responded with many appropriate thank-yous in a practiced way that said she was the type of person who belonged in a glass-walled high-rise office building and got married according to plan. Her mannerisms were poised, practiced into unconscious movements that mimicked the herd. She moved in the circles these women inhabited. She paid for blowouts between hair appointments because they did, and until the pedicure, her place in the group felt secure. The things she collected- clothing and purses, girlfriends from yoga, and an oversized diamond- were enough to prove to others that she belonged. She was not careless enough to permit them a glimpse of the things she had been made of before, attributes they would look sideways at with pity, and stop inviting her to bottomless mimosa Sunday brunches.

"Are you sure he's the one, Caro?" Emma, the CEO's executive assistant, grasped Caro's hand and looked into her eyes. Caro smiled with her mouth closed, caught off guard. She clenched her jaw, but could not stop her eyes from filling. "Aww, honey, you're so in love you can't help yourself. Here you go, hon." Emma handed her a napkin. Caro blinked and dabbed beneath her eyes.

"Thank you, Emma," Caro responded. "I'm just so…"

"I know, dear. You go on and enjoy the rest of this party. Congratulations to you and Evan."

Caro's polite, gracious autopilot continued until noon when the receptionist began dropping the stray plates and forks into a trashcan, and her coworkers filtered out of the conference room. She was grateful that Evan's extended family had limited the amount of guests she could invite and none of her coworkers received an invitation. Soon she was walking through the parking garage, balancing half a sheet cake in her arms. Later, she would remember little of her mechanical performance at the party, but throwing first the cake, and then her engagement ring, out of the car window on the way home would always stand out in her memory.

§

She was not accustomed to being alone, and the stillness in her apartment was unsettling. Every night, Evan wore large headphones and sat with his back to her, staring into his monitor until long after she went to bed, but he was always physically present. He'd been more distant with her for a few months, often eating dinner at his desk, but neither addressed it. She was preoccupied with wedding planning, and he had an online life a world away from their apartment. She looked toward the empty desk and had a momentary flash of the back of his head beneath a pair of headphones with large, puffy ear cushions. She thought of the slope of his broad shoulders, perpetually rounded into bad posture while he was online. Now, the seat was empty, the computer was missing, and she could only speculate on the reasons why. What did it matter now? The opportunity to love and be loved after a dream wedding was gone.

She stood at the refrigerator with the door open, picking at a cold chicken breast with her fingers. She opened a bottle of wine when the breast was gone and stuffed her wedding dress into the back of her closet before she finished the first glass. The hand-hammered metal napkin rings with their engraved initials clinked together as she dropped them into a trash bag. Next, she crumpled the handmade white crepe paper bouquets that would have adorned either side of the guest book table. She filled three trash bags with the remainder of the failed endeavor and took everything to the trash chute. She felt resigned, rather than enraged, and she finished the bottle sooner than she expected to.

She opened a second bottle of wine without looking at the clock, tucked her feet beneath her on the couch, and began to send text messages to her half of the guest list. Her ringer was set to silent, and she did not reply to anyone as the responses began to fill her screen.

§

The maintenance man stood at her door on Friday morning. He thrust the folded seating chart toward her. The stiff board was cracked in three places where she'd bent it to fit into the trash chute. A long, maroon stain had dripped down one of the panels, marring the flourished "Mr. and Mrs. Wheatley" at the top.

"Blocked the trash chute. I seen your names on it. Did you mean to throw this away? Looks like you need this for tomorrow." She took the folded sign from him without speaking and closed the door. Her insides felt heavy. It was too early to open a bottle of wine.

§

She paced the apartment for the rest of the day because she did not know what else to do. The expansive, floor-to-ceiling windows let in the sun, and the pale yellow walls created a warm glow that had once felt welcoming. Today, it felt empty. She looked at the avocado hand-woven Tibetan rug beneath the chrome and glass coffee table and at the framed Matisse print hanging over the couch. These were her items, as was the couch, the bookshelves that lined an entire wall, and the collection of French copper-bottomed cookware hanging from the pot rack in the kitchen. Nothing in the apartment belonged to Evan, not even the computer desk. His name was not on the lease, and they did not have joint accounts. She wondered how he had become so enmeshed in her life without actually integrating himself. He'd opened up such vast possibilities for her to become someone, then departed like a shadow you're sure you saw, but could not describe when questioned. She tried not to wonder where he was. He had not returned her calls or texts. He was not there, and he was not coming back.

It was easy to manage the stigma of being left at the altar in her thirties. The women in her family were accustomed to hardship, damaged marriages, and broken commitments. Before meeting Evan, she separated herself from those women. Even the child she'd been who wore shoes patched with duct tape was long gone. She was successful at a Washington, DC consulting firm. Her taste and style were curated so meticulously that no one would believe a word of her impoverished upbringing. She was partial to expensive, imported handbags, and the yoga pants she wore to the organic market cost more than she would have admitted to either of her sisters. To compare Evan's white picket fence upbringing to hers was to look upon a continuous length of rusty, uneven chain link in a legacy of poverty, hunger, and inadequacy.

The gate on the fence of her childhood screeched or mostly stuck. Evan's whitewashed fence was bordered by manicured flower beds. Hers caught trash that blew against it in the wind, and weeds grew at its base. He knew a little about her past, but she rarely spoke of it. Instead, she spent her salary to separate herself from it so distinctly that it might have been something she heard on NPR and described to him over sushi.

Although ruined dreams and severed promises were bred into her, it was not as easy to manage the abruptness of being single. Marriage to someone like Evan meant the person she'd become, someone with a favorite boutique and season tickets to the theater, was a real self, not a fabrication. Convincing a well-bred man to accept her validated the costume she slipped into years ago and had not removed since they met. However, the marriage was off. Maybe he realized he had more in common with the woman she believed she was than with the girl who didn't always have running water? Evan's parents donated presents to charity at the holidays that parents like hers lined up for. Her family was not even of the ilk to work for a family like the Wheatleys. Why had it taken him a year-long engagement to realize this?

She sprawled on the couch and tapped Evan's entry on her speed dial. It rang four times before the voicemail answered. She did not know what to say so she hung up. She remembered the way you used to be able to answer a caller who was leaving a message on an answering machine. She envisioned a landline ringing and Evan running toward the phone from another room in his parents' spacious home. She thought of words she could have said when Evan answered the phone and interrupted her message; breathless, tearful sentiments about love and promises for the future together, if only they could go through with the wedding. She had not even considered leaving a message like that and the sudden weight of this made her chest ache.

Designer outfits, regular visits to a salon with an unpronounceable name, and twice-weekly appointments with a personal trainer were boxes to check off. The engagement ring was a glittering credential that snagged her hair but garnered entry to a world she knew she did not belong in. The wedding was a final authentication of her success. These things were not the most devastating loss. Without Evan and an impassioned voicemail to reconcile everything, a chance at love, a desire previously kept so close to her chest that it had almost disappeared, was destroyed.

Now, she did not want to think about love or what it took to get the right kind. She did not want the kind that came with voices raised in anger, or the unpredictability of a Friday night on payday when there was more beer than food in the refrigerator. Instead, she wanted what would follow the dream wedding when the man who kissed her at the altar put his arms around her, and she could settle into the knowledge that she did, in fact, deserve to be who she had become. Without the wedding to make this a reality, the only conclusion she could arrive at was the proof of her failure.

By Friday evening, she dismissed her notions of love and missed him as a validation rather than as a fiancé. He was gone, and she owned little else to prop up her facade. She'd purchased diamond earrings and an Italian espresso maker on her own, but Evan was a real person to corroborate her value. Her belongings could not do that, and his abrupt departure felt like a prominent "I told you so." Now, there was nothing to separate her from the neighborhood she grew up in, where every trailer had the number for a bail bondsman taped to the refrigerator. There was little in her apartment to prove that she was not doomed to drive home to her father's single-wide and curl up in the childhood bed she shared with her older sister. She remembered the faint scent of mildew that rose from the mattress even when the sheets were clean, and she shuddered.

She could neither point her car in that direction or that of downtown's Galleria at Fashion Pointe. She did not belong in either of those places. Her stomach felt like it held a tight, hot stone. How many lives was she expected to create before one fit, and she was allowed to settle into it? Her attempt at the one in which you get a diamond engagement ring and a happily ever after had failed. Maybe Evan had seen her fakery and realized the truth. Maybe he left for another reason entirely, but he was gone all the same.

§

On Saturday morning she lay in bed, considering that she would not gather her wedding dress and drive to the ceremony. She did not want to think past that to what else would not happen in her future. She'd been so fixated on the wedding that she felt directionless without a momentous event to focus on. Grooming herself into the woman Evan proposed to had been exhausting, but there had been too much at stake to let things slip. Her engagement ring, then the creamy letterpress save-the-date cards embossed with dragonflies, were tangible measures of her success, and she was finally able to throw herself into something. Planning a wedding was nothing more than tracking details and checking boxes, far less complex than planning a persona.

Now, she was adrift, not even the same person who obsessed over the seating chart and first dance. Her mind drifted to what she might do instead, on what was no longer the biggest day of her life. The apartment was too quiet. The sprawling beach house honeymoon in the Outer Banks was paid in full, and the reservation was not refundable. What would it hurt to take a summer vacation alone?

§

The GPS's voice brings her back to the driver's seat, I-95 South toward the Outer Banks, the empty beach house. She glances at her gas gauge. A few moments later, she merges behind an eighteen-wheeler, likely exiting toward the American 48 Truck Stop. She rounds the cloverleaf exit ramp and follows the road toward the sprawling parking lot. The truck veers toward the "Trucks Only" area in the rear, and she steers toward the expanse of gas pumps.

She considers the other travelers as she fills her tank. Some are pumping gas. Others are washing their windshields or stretching their legs near their vehicles. A scowling teenage boy with a bright shock of acne on his cheeks leads a leashed black and tan mutt from a camper van toward the grass beyond the parking lot. A shrill woman's voice calls to the boy from inside the van, "Do you have poop bags?" He keeps walking and holds his hand out in a thumbs-up gesture. Neither the boy nor the dog look back. She imagines a road trip with a dog, stopping at rest stops to play ball and go potty in the grass. Caro thinks back to the blond ponytail in the shiny, blue convertible. That was a woman who probably owned a dog. Maybe Caro will visit the animal shelter when she gets home. She can be the kind of person who owns a dog.

The gas nozzle's full tank slam ends her reverie, and she tightens the cap with two clicks before slipping into the driver's seat. Her hand grasps the key in an automatic motion, but she pauses and places it on the wheel instead. She is not ready to open the front door of the vacant beach house and have to decide what comes next. She considers the minivan with the "Tucker Tigers" sticker. The driver is probably sure of their destination. The honor roll student is likely to be confident, or at least hopeful, about being on the honor roll again. The eighteen-wheelers filling their tanks at the tall diesel pumps know where they're heading after they rest at this placeless American 48 along their route. She glances at the large, dusty white pickup truck at the pump opposite her. JLC Excavation is stenciled on the side in block lettering, and two men in yellow safety vests sit in the cab. One eats a hotdog from a paper wrapper, and the other holds a Styrofoam coffee cup. A third stands at the gas pump with his hand on the nozzle. She is sure these men have wives at home, or maybe girlfriends, custody issues, and back child support payments due.

Everyone Caro looks at seems confident in their next move, and she feels very small and alone. She cannot start her car because she does not want to bring to life the lonely, silent image of herself in the Outer Banks. A horn honks and she looks in the rearview mirror. Two cars wait in line behind her. She turns the key in the ignition, navigates away from the gas pump, and finds a parking space near the truck stop's entrance.

A river of foot traffic flows through American 48's entrance. People enter, hold the doors, pass the open doors to one another, and pause for slower customers. Others exit with plastic bags in their hands or bags looped over their forearm, holding soda or coffee cups in their hands. Some hold tight to small children's hands while their older children hold the door. Most are dressed for summer vacation. Caro watches the ebb and flow for a moment. She knows humans are flawed and that everyone is not working from a master plan that eludes her, but she cannot get past one thing. Everyone, she believes, has pulled into the American 48 for a reason far more valid than her own. Her eyes follow a woman entering the store. She is close to Caro's age, wearing cheap, purple flip flops, cutoff denim shorts, and a pink tank top. Her hair is bleached into an artificial, yellow blond, curled at the ends with two inches of dark roots at the top. How easy it would be, Caro thinks, to change places with this woman, relax into her world, slip into the passenger seat, and be carried away to someone else's destination. Let this stranger take Caro's place and figure out what to do with an empty beach house and an empty apartment.

She remembers a reliable childhood escape where she could do just that. She had an affinity for stories about children who unexpectedly swapped bodies with others, awoke startled in a strange bed, and had to navigate the school day without letting the grownups know. Her daydreams were filled with deliberate strategies that began with opening her eyes in a new bedroom and passing herself off as someone else's daughter when the new mother served a hot breakfast and kissed her goodbye before school. The new bedroom was always in a clean, comfortable house with a roof that did not leak. She never considered the alarm another child might feel, waking up next to her older sister, discovering pale, grey mushrooms on slender stalks growing behind the toilet, or seeing their breath on winter mornings when there was no money for oil to heat the trailer.

§

Inside American 48, the twang and bass of upbeat country music competes with a low, constant hum of voices. Fluorescent lighting gives off a bright, artificial glow. She slows as she enters and a man knocks into her shoulder in a hurry to exit. She steps to the side, backing into a man filling a to-go box with fried chicken from a small buffet table. "Pardon me, I'm so sorry," she says to the man's back.

He glances toward her, then fixes his attention on the buffet again. He reaches toward a display of sizzling rollers with shiny hot dogs and plump fried tamales rolling under a plastic sneeze guard. She has not eaten food like this in a long time. She pauses for a moment, watching as he deposits a tamale next to a chicken breast in the to-go box. His dark jeans are a little too long, bunched up over the tops of his brown work boots. He wears a red and blue plaid shirt with the cuffs rolled to just below his elbows, tucked in to reveal a wide, brown leather belt. She can make out a rectangular belt buckle, but not what is on it.

"Not much traffic today," she says to the man. From

the side, his tanned face appears kindly. She pictures him behind the wheel of a tractor-trailer, smiling down at children in passing vehicles, honking his horn in response to their tiny crooked arms, raising and lowering from the back seat.

"Beach traffic, this time a' year you can't avoid it. I go where they need me, traffic or not," he responds, placing the tongs next to the tamales and looking toward her.

"What do you drive?"

"Heavy-duty wrecker, some twenty years now." The image of him as a gentle, horn-honking grandfather is replaced with flashes of men in jeans and tee shirts standing on the side of the road next to stranded trucks with their hoods up, and front wheels held high in the air behind enormous wreckers.

She scrambles to find a place for herself in his world. It is not too far of a stretch to imagine kissing a wrecker driver goodbye every morning, then watching the massive vehicle crunch along their gravel driveway toward the next call. She imagines calling a man like this dad, and somehow owning memories of childhood dinners spent listening to his stories of helping truckers on the interstate. He would have been a hero in her eyes, a man who kept the trucks running through every season's beach traffic.

She realizes she has not responded to the trucker, and he is now on the other side of the buffet. The smell of fried foods is overwhelming, so she moves toward a section with clothing racks. Colorful, strappy sundresses hang next to a display of tee shirts with bald eagles soaring into the bright blue sky that covers the shirt's shoulders. She reaches out to grasp a sundress. The fabric is thin and rough, and a few loose threads hang from the neckline. She considers the act of buying a dress from a truck stop. The type of woman who marries a man like Evan would enter American 48, go straight to the restroom, purchase a bottle of mineral water, and walk out. Caro is no longer the type of woman who marries a man like Evan, so she picks through the dresses to find her size. She folds a blue-and-white dress in a patchwork pattern over her arm and turns to take in the rest of American 48.

The music is interrupted by a voice over the crackling speaker, "Customer thirty, your shower is ready. Please proceed to shower number four. Customer thirty-one, your shower is ready. Please proceed to shower number one." The music resumes.

There is a TV lounge along the back wall beyond the expanse of coolers that hold bottled drinks and beer in six-packs and cases. She sees a row of big-screen televisions and the wide, black bar of closed captioning running along the bottom of each one. Four roomy tan leather couches fill the lounge, but it is empty. Beyond that, a large sign over a hallway bears the symbols for restrooms and showers. She adjusts her purse's strap on her shoulder, remembering the twinge of guilt she felt last year at spending so much money on a single accessory. Her fingers pause on the strap, knowing most women who own purses like that do not shower at truck stops. She looks down at the blue dress folded over her arm, understanding that she is not too many years removed from buying clothing at a truck stop or eating tamales on rollers. At this moment, she feels closer to the cheaply made sundress and bald eagle tee shirts than she does to her purse, her apartment in the city, and the job she is not sure how to go back to.

She moves away from the clothing toward the toy aisle. Barbie-sized dolls and cap guns wrapped in plastic hang on bright cardboard backing. The top shelf holds huge stuffed pandas wearing cowboy hats, and the shelves beneath the bears are stocked with plastic blocks in plastic cases. The aisle is filled with generic gifts fathers might bring home to children they rarely see and do not know. The end of the aisle holds a tall, mirrored glass display case filled with crystal pendants and colorful figurines of ballerinas and flowers. "Buy Genuine Crystallina for Those You Love" is engraved on the mirror above the top shelf. The next aisle holds truck supplies, but she cannot identify what the coiled wires, plastic jugs of liquid, and various metal tools are for. She pauses at a display of American 48-branded mud flaps. The red and yellow logo is spotless, and they are so much larger up close than they appear on the backs of eighteen-wheelers. A rack of souvenir "Virginia is for Lovers" mugs and keychains occupies the end cap. She narrows her eyes, taking in the red heart in place of the letter V in the word lovers, and steps out of that aisle toward the registers.

She realizes she is rubbing the fabric of the dress between her fingers but finds that she does not mind its coarseness. She wanders the rest of the aisles, holding the dress to her chest as though it might slip from her grasp. It feels like an anchor point, an object that might help her define herself. Her hefty engagement ring is long gone. The Outer Banks is an ending, rather than a beginning. These symbols, and many more like them from her life with Evan, feel fraudulent and empty. Somehow, the dress does not. The woman who wears this dress can face a group of eager, smiling, judgmental coworkers who want to know how she enjoyed the honeymoon.

The lines at the register are long but moving efficiently. Twice more, she hears the announcement for the showers as she shuffles forward. She pictures herself as customer twenty-six, toting a towel and a change of clothing into shower number eight, and also as the cashier speaking into the microphone. She knows neither wears Manhattan Red on their toenails from a useless pre-wedding pedicure, and both know where they are going when they back out of their parking spaces and guide their vehicles onto the highway.

"I'm sorry, ma'am," says the young cashier, barely out of high school, as she changes places with an older cashier holding a cash drawer. "Shift change." The young cashier has dozens of black and copper braids coiled atop her head above her American 48 visor.

Caro nods and lays the dress on the counter. The older cashier, with a ruddy face and curly, grey hair that rises untamed above her visor, inserts a key into the register and begins pecking on the keyboard. She removes the key, reinserts it, and taps the keyboard again. "I'm sorry we got a little jam here. It'll only be a minute." Caro runs her fingernails through her hair, considering whether a bun or a ponytail would be more comfortable in an American 48 visor.

"Put in your code, do the key, then let me put in mine. I seen Janey do it like that day before yesterday when it stuck." The younger cashier's voice is quick and clipped as she glances at Caro.

"You gotta account for it being my drawer. I'll get it." The older cashier looks at Caro and points to the other cashier, a pale, heavyset man whose bald head shines with sweat above the band of his visor. "You want I can get Jimmy to ring you up over there?"

"Take your time, I'm not in a hurry," Caro responds. She does not want to make either woman uncomfortable. She smiles at them with her lips closed, then looks downwards at the counter. She is glad for the delay because she does not want to get back in the car.

§

How has she missed the sign next to the register? Her heartbeat feels like a hammer and her stomach flutters. She grasps the strap of her purse with one hand and squeezes the dress with the other. Her hands begin to shake, and she does not know what to do with them. She rereads the sign, "Now Hiring Smiling Faces. Ask for an Application Today."

She exhales through pursed lips. This is it, she thinks. This is the way you wake up as a new person and navigate a life you don't have to make up. This help-wanted sign in a middle-of-nowhere Virginia truck stop is how you never have to explain the word "canceled" to your coworkers. This is how you meet people who don't care how you grew up. This is how you wear a backless wedding dress without getting your tattoo removed. Caro glances at the other customers in line. Some are well-dressed. Some are in comfortable traveling clothing. Others appear to earn a living using the strength of their hands and bodies. None are looking at her extravagant purse, her overpriced shoes, or the blue sundress to size up her value. These people are not judging me, she thinks. These are not the Evan Wheatleys of the world, and neither am I. She has two credit cards in her purse and a comfortable savings that will be more than enough. What has she even saved for, if not the ability to make a choice out of desire, rather than necessity?

Jimmy leans into the microphone and calls for customer forty-one to proceed to shower number nine. "Is this all for you, ma'am?" Caro looks up. The older cashier is touching Caro's sundress with one hand, and the younger cashier is carrying her cash drawer toward the back of the truck stop.

Caro straightens her shoulders and makes eye contact with the cashier. She smiles, and responds, "Just the dress, and can I also please have an application?"

South of the Border

Eli and his daughter Pony sit in a rental car in the Target parking lot. He rolls the windows down and turns off the engine. He is not ready to go in. Pony murmurs and taps her tablet in the back seat. He glances at her in the rearview mirror. The sun brings blonde highlights to her hair, and her eyebrows and lashes appear golden in the light. His heart clenches. She looks so small in her booster seat. Xylophone notes rise from her tablet. She giggles, and he watches her for a few moments, glad for the distraction.

§

He received a text from his agent two months ago that a publisher accepted his proposal for a book on depression-era shanty boats in the Gulf states. He forwarded the text to his wife Allie right away. She was meeting potential wedding photography clients, and he wanted her to see the message before she accepted a contract with the bride-to-be. When she responded after the meeting, she was excited to relocate and bring a southern element to her buttoned-up mid-Atlantic photography portfolio. Pony would not start school for another year, so moving south for his research would not be too disruptive.

Now, when he thought of that text, it made his stomach hurt. Could he blame the incident on his agent for pitching the right publisher at the right time? If not for his agent, they would have had no reason to travel south on I-95 that weekend. Instead, he might have pitched something to a local east coast publisher about the Chesapeake Bay. The blue crab population was declining, and Tangier Island was disappearing due to rising sea levels. This would have kept them in Maryland.

He believed that with concentration, he could find the right thing to blame. Someone or something would be brought to justice because there were no other suspects. There were no security cameras in the lot where Allie had to park the U-Haul, which blocked the area from anyone's view. There were no witnesses, only Allie lying silent and broken in the ICU, a U-Haul with a damaged padlock, and three torn cardboard moving boxes that were found with their contents scattered but not stolen. Visualizing the fugitives was like looking into a camera's flash; indelible blinding brightness, followed by darkness and a permanently ghosted image on your retinas that does not fade with blinking. It was difficult to transform the faceless perpetrators from shadow and smoke into something tangible to focus his anger on. Sometimes, Eli extended his index finger into a nervous divining rod of blood and bone and tapped things as though the rhythm could identify the guilty party. This was all he had.

§

He grasps his phone from the passenger's seat in the Target parking lot and opens a news app. He is not sure what will make him feel ready to go in. Last month's nationwide Amber Alert recently ended in tragedy. Every news outlet is vying for the story du jour. The public is insatiable for details about cherubic nine-year-old Angela Parker, with a round, babydoll face, bangs, and bright green eyes. Politics and global warming are momentarily forgotten because Angela the Angel's face is everywhere. It is too easy to find a story like hers in every state when you start looking into local news across the country. He has too much time on his hands now, and he has obsessed over this since the thing with Allie. There are Angelas of every age, from infants to girls like Pony, to college girls Pony might grow into. There are stories about women like Allie. There are grandmothers. Senior citizens, for Christ's sake. Who would even… He pushes the thought away and notices he is gripping his phone too tightly.

§

In his desperation to blame something other than himself, he pointed his divining rod at South of the Border, the sprawling roadside attraction off I-95 in South Carolina. There were so many opportunities for accusations that he could get lost in them. He began with the colorful billboards, ubiquitous along the interstate many miles from the property. On their southbound road trip, they decided to stop there for the night after seeing the third one. Allie turned to Pony who was sitting between them in the U-Haul in her booster seat, and asked, "Have you ever seen a horse wearing a sombrero?" The billboards became a game with each of them trying to call out that they'd spotted it first. He fumed, remembering the other billboards they passed. Why hadn't Allie decided on the Holiday Inn? They had a pool and a free hot breakfast. Fuck those festive billboards.

Next to blame were the margaritas at South of the Border's Mexican restaurant, where they ate after checking into their room. Their margaritas were a disappointing neon blend of cheap sour mix and inferior tequila, rimmed with table salt. Neither of them was able to drink more than a few tentative swallows. After dinner, Allie snapped a few pictures of Pony smiling wide and posing in front of an enormous concrete dachshund. They visited the gift shop, and as promised, Allie bought Pony a plastic horse wearing a red, green, and yellow sombrero.

"I could really use a drink," Eli said once they were settled in their room. Allie was running her fingertips over Pony's head, smoothing her newly cropped, light brown hair. A few days before leaving Baltimore, both of his girls came home with matching pixie cuts. Allie said the south's humidity wouldn't agree with their fine, wavy hair, and it was probably time for an update anyway.

"I could use a drink, too," Allie responded. "If you finish putting Pony to bed, I'll run out. You've been driving all day."

He did not want to get back into the U-Haul, and he handed Allie the keys.

When he thought about wanting a drink after the margaritas neither could finish, he cursed the margaritas. It was easy to place a fierce and furious blame on the bartender or the waitress. He tried to focus on the table, two mostly full goblets with melting ice, floating lime wedges, and the salted rim dripping downwards in watery rivulets. He thought of his plate, a pool of uneaten refried beans next to a pile of orange rice dotted with tiny carrot cubes and wrinkled peas. They should have ordered Coronas with dinner. This would have changed everything.

They would have stayed at the table drinking and picking at the basket of chips. They would have talked about tomorrow's drive or Allie's photography ideas using southern oak trees hung with Spanish moss. They would have ordered another round as Pony drew on her paper placemat with crayons or pranced the toy horse between the condiments that she lined up before her. After two beers each, they would have gone back to their room and tucked Pony in. They would have sat in bed next to each other, reading with their thighs touching. They would have turned out the light and nestled into the big and little spoon. If he opened his eyes in the dark, he would have seen the outline of Allie's ear against the parking lot lights coming through the gaps in the curtains.

§

He closes the news app showing Angela the Angel and glances at Pony in the back seat again. She is too young to wonder why they are sitting in a rental car in a Target parking lot with the windows rolled down, both staring at their screens. He opens Facebook, and it greets him with a memory from six years ago. The abrupt weight in his stomach feels like a body, inert and silent.

"Allie: Why are you using the chipped cup?

Me: So you don't have to.

Allie: But I always use the chipped cup so YOU don't have to."

§

He handed his wife the keys to the U-Haul. She kissed the top of Pony's head. She looped her purse over her shoulder and stood on her toes to plant a kiss on his mouth. She opened the door and closed it behind her. He heard the U-Haul's engine start a moment later. He changed into sweatpants. He read Pony three storybooks and put her to bed. He used the toilet. He washed his hands. He straightened Pony's toys. He read a long-form article on *The New Yorker's* website about celebrity influencers on Adderall. He looked at his phone, but there were no messages. He looked at the red numbers on the clock radio on the nightstand.

He picked up his phone, typed, "liquor store near me," into the search, and calculated the time it would take to drive a U-Haul three miles to the closest town with a liquor store. There were other liquor stores nearby. She would not have gone too far without a text. He pressed her name on speed dial. Her phone rang until the voicemail picked up. He hung up and looked at Pony. Her breathing was slow and relaxed. He tapped out a quick, "Where are you?" and pressed send. There was no reply. He opened and closed two different news apps. He dialed her phone, leaving a message this time. He opened and closed the news apps again. He sent another text. He looked at the clock radio. He looked at his unanswered texts. Allie had been gone for over an hour.

§

His eyes begin to prick with tears at the six-year-old Facebook memory about a chipped cup, but they do not fill. He drops his phone onto the passenger's seat. Facebook, he seethes. Fuck Facebook. He runs his fingers across an eyebrow, glancing in the rearview mirror again. He is making the right decision in this Target parking lot. He tightens his grip on his phone, believes he has considered all angles and found nothing suitable, save for this idea that he'll share with Allie when he can. When the idea hit him, watching Pony play with her plastic animal toys in an extended-stay hotel suite near the hospital, he knew this was the best choice.

"You ready to go get some stuff?"

"Okay, Daddy. Let's go. Did you know there's a purple man on here?" Pony responds, holding her tablet toward him.

"Ohh, I see that. Shut it down and let's go in."

§

When he tried to blame South of the Border, it felt like he was spinning a rigged wheel at a cheap, parking lot carnival. Each space on the wheel designated culpability, and if he spun the wheel properly, the guilty party would come to light. Instead, the wheel's arrow landed on his last words to his wife, "I could really use a drink." His agent was doing his job. They could have ignored the alluring billboards along I-95. The waitress brought margaritas because they ordered them. He could not even visualize the culprits, and the police had no leads. Every time he let the wheel spin, he watched in horror as it clicked to a stop with the vicious and haunting arrow of guilt pointed directly at himself. He knew this was irrational. However, he kept the wheel spinning, willing it to land on someone other than himself.

Pony often rescued him from these finger-pointing, jaw-clenching deliberations. A few days after they checked into the hotel, rented a car, and parked the U-Haul in the hotel's back parking lot, he saw her standing before him. She was bouncing the hard, brown hooves of her favorite tan horse on his thigh. "Daddy, are you okay? Do you want to play with us?" She held the horse toward him. He blinked and took in the suite's placelessness. They could be anywhere from Alaska to Chicago. The suite spoke of limbo; the furnishings were sturdy but not well-made, and he could not imagine any person owning these items. You could fill the refrigerator and unpack your suitcase, but your clothing in the drawers would not make you feel at home.

He had no idea how long she'd been there, running the horse up and down his leg. He moved from the dated leather couch to the carpet and sat amidst a menagerie of six-inch plastic animals. He held a spotted giraffe in one hand and a zebra in the other.

Pony was setting up the rest of the zoo in two rows along a tan stripe on the carpet. "Daddy, these ones are the boys, and these ones are the girls." She placed her favorite horse in the boy's row. "You put yours here," she said, gesturing toward the girl's row. An idea struck him. He looked at her small, oval face and faint eyebrows. Short, fine hair framed her forehead. Her tiny pale pink ears, no larger than seashells, were not pierced. She identified Pony the horse as a boy. Pony Boy.

Once, in their Baltimore apartment, Pony brought the horse to breakfast and asked for oats because the horse, aptly named Pony, wanted oats for breakfast. On this day, his daughter Melissa became Pony. Allie leaned over and whispered to him, "Can we just call her Pony Boy," referencing a character in *The Outsiders,* an old book they both coincidentally read in fifth grade. They made conspiratorial eye contact and turned up the corners of their mouths in the shared inside joke their daughter would never understand. Allie would never have planned for this trip to Target, yet her comment conceived of it perfectly.

Pony could pull him from an abyss in which he lost himself to his thoughts, but she could not rescue him from the mirrors in their suite. It felt cruel and shameful to look at the reflection of a man whose one job, seated within the most primitive part of his brain, was to protect his family.

Instead, he disregarded that tenet so flagrantly that he felt he could no longer occupy his own image. His reflection appeared distorted with a disgrace that made his throat constrict, and he did not recognize the rictus of helplessness that masked his face.

He assigned blame to so many parts of his body that he did not recognize them either; his mouth told his wife to drive away from their hotel room; his hands gave her the keys; his lips kissed her goodbye; his legs did not run after her when he heard the U-Haul's engine start. He stopped shaving to avoid looking at the features on a face that no longer resembled the man he once was. He washed his hands and brushed his teeth in the kitchenette. Sometimes he could not even turn on the bathroom light. He could not bear to look at the man in the mirror.

Pony did not ask why he hung a sheet over the mirror above the dresser. The sheet hid the warped web of shattered acrylic mirror that he punched once when she was asleep. By Allie's fourth day in ICU, uncharacteristic stubble sprouted from his jawline, chin, and neck. His eyes were puffy and more red than white. This was not a man he knew or wanted to be seen with. This was a man who deserved to be punched in the middle of his silver, wire-rimmed glasses. He did just that, enraged at the incompetent, powerless animal standing before him. There was no good answer to why the sheet was there, and he was glad she had not asked.

§

Eli holds Pony's hand as he steers her across the parking lot. He looks down at her pink and white shoes. No more pink. They will head to the shoe department first.

He can almost hear himself telling Allie about this plan. He imagines her nodding and agreeing that there is no way around it, and both of them wholly believing this. He presumes they will both stand behind this idea when she comes home. Together, they will arrive at a long-term plan.

§

Allie's condition stabilized over the course of a week that lasted a decade. She was not out of the woods. However, they assured him she was going to make it. They did not say when she would "make it," or even what the words "make it" meant. They did not say what would happen after she "made it," or what would transpire between husband and wife after they discharged her. What did "make it" look like to a woman assaulted into unconsciousness with such brutality that the medical team used platitudes like miracle and guardian angel when describing her inexplicable survival?

The shift nurses took pity on him. The ICU visiting hours for children Pony's age were limited, and he was not comfortable finding a local sitter. It was against the rules, but they allowed Pony to sit in a chair behind the nurse's station with her tablet while Eli spent time at Allie's bedside. It was hard for him to look at her, but it was harder to look away.

In the first few days, it felt like there was no time to think, but it was not really about time at all. Instead, it was about reacting to the basest instinct to wish for life over death. He had not been given this choice. However, he felt he might be able to control the outcome if only he drew the right conclusions about their future together. This sucked moments from his hours and hours from his days.

He discovered that Pony's small tablet, once used sparingly, worked as a babysitter, and he did not feel guilty letting her watch Disney movies for hours uninterrupted while he brooded.

To choose life, and to will that Allie made a full recovery, was to believe he could have her back in the moments before he said, "I could really use a drink." He envisioned their life returning to normal in their new home. Baltimore would live in their memories on one side of a fat, black line dividing their lives into distinct halves. The book about shanty boats would eventually sit on their bookshelf. Allie's photography business would flourish. Pony, whomever she grew up to be, would thrive. There was no other option than to choose this for his wife and their future together.

However, he could not silence a nagging inner voice that said their life on the gulf would never resemble normalcy. When Allie "made it," the voice said she would not settle back into the woman he married, or return to anything close to herself. The voice had lots to say about who he would become to her. How would she react the first time he reached toward her to hold her hand? What had she done with her hands when the men approached her in the darkened parking lot of Duke's Fine Liquors? The first time he wanted to embrace her, he was uncertain whether her body would even permit the sensation of a man's arms encircling her. The fat, black line would define them forever after.

He considered how to still the familiar arousal he felt for her when Pony's door was closed for the night. He thought of making love to her after she "made it." He was not able to get past the mechanics of the act. There was an insurmountable gulf between his intentions and the catastrophic damage that had been done. Other men defiled his wife's body as he sat in a hotel room waiting for a bottle of bourbon. The idea of it made his skin feel too tight, and he wanted to crawl out of it. Sometimes, he needed to shake his head and force the air from his lungs in a sharp exhalation to clear those thoughts from his head.

He was not sure how to touch her or whether it was best to let her touch him first. What if she never did? He feared that lovemaking would become something he inflicted on her. She would lie beneath him, and he would not know the thoughts and feelings that flashed through her mind.

He imagined her face the last time they made love in their Baltimore apartment. Sunday morning sunlight filtered through the thin, white curtains. He paused for a moment on top of her and looked into her eyes. When he uttered the words "I love you so Goddamn much," she pulled him toward her and kissed him. He tried to picture that scene in a new home on the gulf, but her eyes were rimmed with red, and her face was wet with tears. He imagined rolling to his side of the bed, not knowing how to form an apology that included both their bedroom at that moment and handing her the keys to the U-Haul.

When Allie's condition in the ICU was grave and uncertain, the sinister voice that was not his own did not choose life. It said Baltimore was their time, and he would forever be relegated to remembering her in the past tense. There would be no "made it." She would become a lonely, "those were the days" memory. He would tell Pony the good parts when she no longer remembered her mother, and he would not have to look at the woman who left their hotel room because he did not feel like driving.

§

There is a thin, oily-looking man in dirty jeans and a stained tee shirt eyeing the display of $1 items at Target's entrance near the shopping carts. His boots are worn away at the toes, showing glints of dull, reinforced steel beneath the leather. Eli grips Pony's hand a bit tighter and quickens their steps. He makes eye contact with the man as they pass to flash a warning: "I know what you are." He knows he would not have thought this in Baltimore. There have been more Amber Alerts on the East Coast within the last five days. Four, still active and unsolved, were little girls. One, a boy, was kidnapped by his father, but he was found safely twenty-four hours later.

§

Eli conceived of a dark fantasy in which he was free of the burdens of guilt, blame, and single fatherhood. In a world only slightly different than this one, Allie and Pony could have suffered any number of disastrous, permanent tragedies. He would be a man who had it all and lost everything. In that grim fabrication, there would be nothing left to lose. Thinking of this made him feel powerful and dangerous when he let the carnival wheel of blame spin in his thoughts for too long.

There was no book on shanty boats in the alternate world. There was no apartment or hometown. There was only the road and a long, low car with a deep, growling muffler. He would have a machete in the back seat, and guns in a guitar case. There would be cheap roadside motor courts, dive bars and pool halls, and men who never saw him coming. He would not merely dole out justice to men who caused pain and tore families apart. That was too simple.

Instead, he would make his own rules, bending the laws of physics to suit himself. He would suss out and eliminate the men with rotten, wormy intentions to commit future acts. First, the shadows in his mind would form themselves into the men responsible for Allie's condition. He would see them in daylight and look into their eyes, but not to seek a reason for their violence. Instead, he wanted his face to be the last thing they saw. He played out the scenario using the guns in the guitar case or the machete. One weapon first and then the other, and vice versa, and then each weapon alone. He would never get blood on his clothing. They would be ineffectual against his rage, and he would become a monster who ate other monsters.

§

Eli and Pony pass the home improvement section on their way to the toys. He attempts to make eye contact with every man they pass. A man with a black soul, moments from causing another Amber alert, could be anywhere. A man who has already inflicted damage and torn a family apart could be in this very store. They look like everyone else until you see their guilty, grainy figure on the enhanced security camera footage. There has always been much to protect Pony from, and these things used to be par for the course. Now, the dangers are so much worse.

Danger is a live creature manifested in men who could be looking at a display of knives in housewares with a new six-piece set of cookware in their cart. A man with a basket held in the crook of his elbow may have duct tape and plastic sheeting hidden beneath a box of granola cereal. A cashier might be ringing up industrial-sized garbage bags and bleach along with deodorant and a three-pack of white men's tube socks.

Allie's path crossed with men like this. If not for this shopping trip to begin the grand safekeeping stratagem, Pony's path would cross with them as well.

Eli knows little boys disappear, but he believes there are far fewer instances than girls. He has seen alerts and read news stories about boys, but they barely register. He played outside after sunset with his brothers during his entire childhood, where "stranger danger" was only connected to Halloween candy. He did not grow up looking over his shoulder, but he knows this is something Allie was taught to do. Women and girls have always been in more danger, and he is ashamed to have forgotten this.

His inaction with Allie caused an irreversible trauma, and she lies in a hospital bed a few miles away because he was not vigilant and watchful. However, he is certain that his plan will stave off Pony's danger. With Allie, he did not even think to look for it. Neither of them did. Why would you think you could not just drive to the liquor store like everyone else? He's now hyper-aware of how great the peril is for little girls, so he will guide Pony toward the necessary items on his shopping list. He believes Allie will pull through. He will convince her that this is the best arrangement, just for now. Just until Allie is a whole person again, and they settle in a new state far from the damages of South of the Border. Together, they will figure out who Allie and Pony are to become.

"Daddy, can I get a ball?" There is a cage of rubber bouncy balls on an endcap. A ball will be perfect. She reaches through the large opening and grasps a lavender ball as large as her head.

He pulls a blue ball from the cage. "Blue's the best one," he says, and she giggles, showing her milk teeth. They exchange colors and she tosses the blue ball in the air. It bounces down the aisle and she runs after it laughing. In three urgent, breathless strides he has caught up to her. He reaches down, catches her arm near her armpit and jerks her toward him. "Pony, no." His words are sharp, unexpected. Her face crumbles into tears. The ball has rolled out of sight. He kneels, wraps his arms around her, presses his face into the top of her head, whispering, "I'm so sorry."

She calms. Her face is pink. Her cheeks are wet and her lashes are matted. "Daddy," she says, her face close to his. "You scared me. Where's the ball?" Together, they hold hands and walk down the aisle with the backpacks and insulated lunch coolers to retrieve the ball. She cradles it to her chest with one arm and they walk toward the front of the store, holding hands. They pass the $1 section. The thin man with worn boots is not there. Eli hoists Pony into a cart and steers it away from the entrance. "Let's go check out the shoes. Whadda ya' say to that?" He winks at her, and she nods with enthusiasm.

In the shoe section, Eli examines a pair of navy blue tennis shoes with orange laces. There is a soccer ball stitched onto the side of each one. He tells her these are special shoes, that the soccer ball will help her run her fastest to keep up with the new blue ball. Her eyes light up with this knowledge. Eli helps her try on three pairs to find the best fit, and she is delighted when he allows her to keep them on her feet. He places her pink and white shoes inside the empty shoebox and secures the lid. He thinks of Allie's joke about *The Outsiders*, Pony Boy. He is so confident she will agree with this that he has not even considered how he will convince her if she doesn't.

He guides the cart past a rack of leggings with pink and turquoise sparkles. They pass a display of dresses next to a rack of pastel tee shirts with cartoon cats and llamas wearing crowns. He turns the cart past a rack of boy's navy blue blazers and khaki pants with sharp creases, and they stop next to a display of folded brown and camouflage pants with reinforced knees. On the left is a rack of superhero tee shirts in bold, primary colors. His fingers move through the pants until he comes to a brown pair with an elastic waistband in Pony's size. He looks over the tee shirts, grasping a small, red one. On the front, Spiderman is crouching, and webs shoot from his wrists. He holds the shirt toward Pony, and she extends her arm to run her fingers along the web. "Spiderman, spiderman," he sings out, bending and reaching an arm toward her in a tickling gesture. "Doing the things a spider can." She squeals and pulls away as his hand tickles her ribs. He looks down at her, so small and fragile before him, and places the brown pants and Spiderman tee shirt in the cart next to the ball.

An elderly woman with a cane totters down the aisle as Eli pushes the cart away from a rack of little boy's sports jackets. He pauses to let her pass. She stops, taking in Pony, who is occupied with her new shoes. "Well, hello there, fellow," she says, looking not at Eli, but at his daughter. Pony, agonizingly shy around strangers, glances toward the woman and looks at her shoes again. His hands grip the cart and his body seems to swell from the inside. His ears fill with the sound of his heartbeat. He is supposed to be in charge of this moment, yet here is a stranger taking the lead. He tries to swallow but his mouth is so dry that he coughs instead, and this propels him back into the boy's section.

He takes in Pony's haircut and delicate features, molded into a visage of childhood androgyny. The woman speaks to Pony again. "How old are you, little mister?" Pony does not look up, and the woman looks to Eli.

They make eye contact, and Eli responds. "He's four."

Eight Story Ideas That Didn't Make It Into This Collection

Story One—The child is defined by negative space, what she doesn't do, what she could've become. As a child, I received photo-sensitive paper. I laid out leaves and flowers to burn into secret shapes while the paper bleached in the sun. What could I have become if my mother had taken that inherited house in Rochester, always a fantasy of escape until I learned the city has one of the highest crime rates in the country. The things I could have become take on a different shape in a city like that. Leave out the inherited house. Tell only of the wonderous negative images on cornflower-blue paper, and the innocence of discovery.

Not every story needs to wrench the heart.

Story Two—"They've taken almost everything," says Pap. "Our land is next." We dig three graves. Mam agrees and I follow. Sometimes we stand at the edges. Pap yells down the driveway into the trees, rehearsing for when the men come. He wants to practice falling into the holes. I picture the flutter of my skirt against my calves. Mam can't abide by scrubbing dirt from our clothing and won't go that far. I've seen enough movies to know it won't be the army coming. It'll be Clem Marsden in a county pickup, come to collect back taxes. Mam says to wait. Pap will get his self picked up in town for the busted taillight, kept overnight for drunkenness. Then, she says, we can leave.

Try to write a story where the mother is the protector. This one is not a memoir.

Story Three—Imagine a bird's nest as you approach the bird. Think hard and desperately of this scene: nest = home. Wish. Pray. Be the safety. Then, it will know you're harmless and not fly away from you. You must know its nest intimately, every stalk and reed woven into a sheltered basket. Picture the eggs unhatched, then the chicks. Hear their peeping. Imagine your feathers, if you had them, brushing against their downy fluff. With this knowledge, the red-winged blackbirds no longer fly away when you pass them in the marsh.
When writing or creating life goals, it's okay to imagine yourself winged and feathered, and never coming back.

Story Four—We stopped on the side of the road somewhere west, summer of '94, going to another Grateful Dead show, or on our way to a Rainbow Gathering on top of a mountain in Flagstaff. I woke early to a brown landscape, sunrise, a buffalo near the wire fence. It was as large as a bus, matted fur, dinner-plate eye. In this story, I'll be alone. The buffalo will say, "Go home." I'll start the car, homebound. On the road, I'll figure out where home is.
I didn't figure out home that summer, but the buffalo made a good story.

Story Five—Picture leaving in the middle of a shift, the feeling of a stranger's rough palm on your bare skin for the last time. Glance down at the bulge of cash in your purse on the passenger seat. Scream at the crack in your windshield. Wonder how much tread is left on your tires. Ease your car onto the highway. You shrink along the way, inexplicably. You welcome it. You get out of the car on the side of the road in the Sonoran desert. Your feet no longer reach the pedals. Your clothes are as big as circus tents.

There's a fine, silky fur covering your skin. Here are the facts: grasshopper mice prey on poisonous scorpions and centipedes. They don't feel pain when they're stung. At night, they tip their noses toward the sky in fierce howls across the barren terrain. Think of inhaling desert air, mimicking their ferocious wail.
Magical realism is a popular genre right now. Consider adding a mouse romance, or a vampire.

Story Six—First, there was a dream of the Salton Sea, its fishy shores and trailer parks. She learned of Slab City in ruins, a settlement for artists and junkies. In the story, her father spoke of royalty, "We used to be kings, now we're remnants," of his long-ago job waiting tables at the Salton Sea resort where The Beach Boys played all summer. She'd hold The Remnants in her mind, driving cross-country to find something of her father.
It's difficult to imagine being someone with a father called Daddy.

Story Seven—This one isn't formed into plot and arc. Instead, it's jagged flashes, not yet a story, the grinding guitar and guttural vocals that know my name and the catalog of damages I've done to myself. There is a *you* in all those old songs from when you damaged, and when you were the damage. The singer drags herself over broken glass for someone. That's the story, what she did for her man. It isn't a story to say there was broken glass I dragged myself over because it was there. It isn't a story to say the scars, and rips, and tears were things I tripped over because I had no one to tell me they weren't a good idea. There's a story about me in the melody and the lyrics, but I'm not ready to tell it.
Tell it. Bare your soul, but use a good title. People respond to

clickbait.

Story Eight—Last, and this will be a good one, tell of the long-ago photos before OnlyFans, the glossy spreads in magazines they sold wrapped in plastic. Tell of having fans before Instagram when there was no way to quantify them. Tell of sharing a table at a convention with a pretty brunette like any other model, long before she married Marylin Manson. Tell of the money and travel. Also, tell of the stage name in lights and the loneliness when the makeup came off. Tell of those years because they're a good story, but say they are fiction.

Don't write this collection. Write a novel instead. Everyone knows that's more marketable.

Acknowledgements

The author would like to thank the editors of the following publications where the following stories have appeared, sometimes in varying forms: "The Box," *Concrete Desert Review*; "The Numbers Man," *Counterclock Journal*; "The Wings That Follow Fear," *Levee Magazine*; "Dating Silky Maxwell," *Meat for Tea: The Valley Review*; and, "Eight Story Ideas That Didn't Make It Into My Collection," *McNeese Review*.

Thank you to my husband, Charles, for being my first reader, encouraging me through terrible first drafts, and providing me with many places and opportunities to write.

Thank you to my beloved editor, Caroline Swicegood. I wouldn't be the writer I am today without you. Thank you to the instructors at The Writer's Center in Bethesda, Maryland who helped shape my words when I was new to taking them seriously: Lynn Auld Schwartz, Kathryn Johnson, and Laura J. Oliver. Thank you to Patricia Henley at the Chesapeake Writer's Conference for first encouraging me to turn my fledgling stories into a collection. Thank you to my early writing group in Chesapeake Beach for reading my words before I knew what I was doing. Thank you to Ann for your valuable early feedback. Thank you to Trudy for providing a damn good writing retreat. Thank you to the entire ELJ Editions family for believing in this collection. Lastly, thank you to all the women and men within these pages; without getting to know you and your gritty, hardscrabble lives, my writing and photography would never have evolved.

About the Author

TJ Butler is a writer and photographer who lives on a sailboat on the Chesapeake Bay. She writes fiction and essays that are not all fun and games, teaches workshops, and coaches writers. Her work has appeared in outlets such as Huffington Post and Insider and a variety of literary journals. She has a degree in a field she will never return to, and she was one of those kids who wanted to be a writer when they grew up. Her black-and-white photography mimics her writing's gritty themes. *Dating Silky Maxwell* is her first collection. Connect with her at TJButlerAuthor.com.